WORDSWORTH

POET OF THE
UNCONQUERABLE MIND

A Collection of Essays

on

Wordsworth's Poetry

by

Bennett Weaver

Edited by

Charles L. Proudfit

The George Wahr Publishing Co.
Ann Arbor, Michigan
1965

PR
5881
.W4

To

Charles Leslie

PREFACE

Fifteen years ago the late Ernest Bernbaum, in a survey of Wordsworthian scholarship, suggested that Bennett Weaver's essays on Wordsworth, written between 1934 and 1940, be collected into a book. Professor Bernbaum states several reasons for his suggestion:

> The approach is psychological, but it is governed by a true sense for the complex nature of imaginative literature; and there is no similarity to the prosaic methods of the strict systematizers. Weaver traces in the life and the poems Wordsworth's aesthetic-religious development—the interrelated functions and phases of sense-experience, affections, memory, reflection, and imagination. Perhaps he overstates the antagonism between sense-experience and imagination, as Francis Christensen asserts in 'Creative Sensibility in Wordsworth' (*JEGP*, 1946); but this does not seriously impair the general soundness of these admirable interpretations. [1]

As a former student of Professor Weaver, I am happy to be able to make "these admirable interpretations" available in book form to scholars and students of Wordsworth's poetry. I have included in this collection, in addition to the essays mentioned by Professor Bernbaum, Bennett Weaver's most recent comment upon Wordsworth, "Wordsworth: Poet of the Unconquerable Mind" (*PMLA*, 1960), an essay which reflects Professor Weaver's unusual ability to appreciate and to deal with transcendental idealism and the difficult, although essential, concepts of Wordsworth.

With the exception of the final essay, "Wordsworth: Poet of the Unconquerable Mind," which has been retyped, all of the essays in this collection appear, with minor non-textual changes, in the exact form of their original publication. The page numbers between dashes are my own, but the pagination of the original journal has been retained.

I should like to thank the editors of the following scholarly publications for granting permission to have these essays reprinted: *Studies in Philology; Papers of the Michigan Academy*

---

[1] Reprinted by permission of the Modern Language Association from *The English Romantic Poets: A Review of Research*, ed. Thomas M. Raysor (New York, 1950), p. 61.

Preface

of Science, Arts, and Letters; Philological Quarterly; and Publications of the Modern Language Association of America. I should like also to thank Professor Richard C. Boys, Professor Arthur M. Eastman, and Professor Warner G. Rice for their helpful advice. For his encouragement and active interest in this project, I should like to express my gratitude to Professor Robert H. Super. Finally, I wish to acknowledge my indebtedness to Professor Bennett Weaver for allowing me to collect these essays.

Charles L. Proudfit

University of Michigan

CONTENTS

Contents

WORDSWORTH'S *PRELUDE*:
AN INTIMATION OF CERTAIN PROBLEMS IN CRITICISM

By Bennett Weaver

In dealing with *The Prelude* of Wordsworth there seems to be a tendency to imply that one must accept as literally true what the poet says about himself before one can know the truth about his poem. No doubt a certain profound veracity in the work betrays the critic. Having sensed this truth of deeper birth, by consequent impulses he declares the record in the poem accurate and completes the paradox by believing implicitly what by faith he first invested with authority.

This is the way of the marvelous in criticism. I wish to raise three questions against it and to suggest that the poetic value of *The Prelude* would not be seriously impaired if all of the answers were derogative to such manipulation. Surely we are on the high street to the misunderstanding of poetry when we first inform it with biographical meaning and then inform ourselves with the poetical meaning derived from the biographical.

We remark the fact that this poet is peculiarly given to contemplating emotion recollected in tranquillity till, " by a species of reaction, the tranquillity gradually disappears, and an emotion, kindred to that which was before the subject of contemplation, is gradually produced, and does itself actually exist in the mind." This *kindred* emotion is not the *original* emotion, but is " qualified by various pleasures " and voluntarily constrained to preserve the " state of enjoyment " about which Nature herself is so " cautious." I submit that the poetic mood so produced, so straitened, and so delivered to a premeditated purpose is in no condition to deal with recollected matters in terms of mere accuracy, but can deal with them only after the profounder veracities of the imagination. So long as criticism can apprehend these veracities—and how far it can I am happy in being under no immediate obligation to indicate—it may depend upon them. But one may doubt that it makes any difference in so far as quintessential poetry is concerned whether the young man is walking away from London or Bristol and whether he steals a boat from among the rushes of Esthwaite or from beneath a willow tree overhanging Ullswater. I do not say that some different degree of curious interest might not manifest itself in the one case or the other; but that interest at best could do little more than postpone our appreciation of the poetry of the poem.

We have, furthermore, come to question the process of recollection even though it be most calm, and even though it do not have to engage in the difficulty of remaining tranquil even while overflooded by powerful feelings. This is, of course, as Wordsworth tells us, what it does not do. For once the emotion begins to flow across the surface of tranquillity, then " tranquillity gradually disappears," and stormy ecstasy may ensue. Whatever this ecstasy is most cunning in, it is not cunning in an ordered setting forth of facts brought up from the stores of memory. How might not a poet tortured and almost physically haunted by " a secret burden " betray accuracy in order in a much profounder way to find relief in betraying himself! Altogether too insistently we are told that the story of a Margaret or an Ellen is from real life and " truly related." We know well that to the very extent of their truth they may be calculated the more safely to serve as masks behind which a suffering man may hide while in confession he relieves his o'erfraught mind. I offer the illustration merely to suggest that one who struggles too hard to withhold a great truth cannot be trusted too implicitly in the little which he succeeds in revealing.

Let us return to *The Prelude*. Wordsworth has been honest and explicit regarding two vital matters. First, he tells us that in writing the poem he is fixing the " wavering balance " of his mind by fetching thoughts from " days Disowned by memory " (I. 360-1). Although many a matter has " Wearied itself out of the memory " (I. 344), his soul " retains an obscure sense of possible sublimity," (II. 317-18) " Remembering how she felt, but what she felt Remembering not " (II. 316-17). I do not wish to labor this point;[1] but I do wish to suggest that here we are not dealing with that kind of memory which records, " I was at Ambleside on June thirteenth and there I drilled thirteen volunteers." This is a higher

---

[1] In the 1850 version the direct uses of the word *memory* are to be found in I. 75, I. 574, I. 598, I. 615, III. 188, III. 299, III. 329, III, 627, IV. 308, V. 198, VI. 659, VII. 335, VII. 366, VII. 464, VII. 509, VII. 741, VIII. 559, IX. 270, IX. 583, XI. 390, XIV. 410.

memory whose function is of the soul; and only in the obscure ways of the soul may we come upon the immaterial records of how the poet felt in "days Disowned by memory." We are here twice removed from factual accuracies, if indeed we are not on another plane entirely. For *what* a soul may feel is surely removed from the factual, and yet even that is denied this higher memory. The soul may remember only *how* she felt. In so far as the poetry of the poem is concerned I should like to indulge a supposition: In fondness and in love Wordsworth recollects—not some fact or happening—rather some old emotion. Upon this old emotion, if he does not utterly absorb it and transmute it by contemplation, the mature poet impinges " obscure feelings representative Of things forgotten" (I. 606-7), often those comprised in a powerfully imagined visionary experience which would have dispersed to atoms the pulpy substances of a child's mind. The boy who stole the boat probably did not feel and doubtless could not have felt the blank desertion strangely full of huge and mighty forms. It is the empowered poet who feels that the boy felt those things. And here may I repeat: there is no other poetry than the poetry of the poem. Obviously I am not trying to assert that the boy did not steal the boat, although in a moment we shall have to raise a question of just such kind.

The second of the vital matters about which Wordsworth has been explicit is that the " heroic argument " of his poem, the dealing with what passed within himself, " in the main lies far hidden from the reach of words " (III. 138-9).[2] He is really involved in the master paradox of his majestically paradoxical mind: he is communicating the " incommunicable." Naturally enough—and no one could be more candid about it—he suffers " Through sad incompetence of human speech." He is brave to confess what Shelley later asserts, that " the deep truth is imageless." It matters not, for purposes of this observation, that Wordsworth may sink deeper and rise higher than any other of the sons of light or that he may succeed in revealing to us more than any other poet has revealed. The point still remains that he cannot find language to tell us of his own majestic uttermost and that in his own opinion there is a failing of the very breath of words as the veils of sublimity fall away before his inspired gaze. Plainly this involves the poetry of the poem; for the reference is not to narrative mat-

[2] Cf. II. 198-232.

ters, but to those supreme poetic moments " when the light of sense Goes out " (VI. 13) and Wordsworth is lost before the glory of the invisible world. I do not wish so much as to intimate that those high poetic experiences which fall within what Wordsworth himself has called " spots of time " in any way controvert the simple narrative statements of *The Prelude*; but I do wish to suggest that it is exactly as great a leap from the narrative matters to the experiences of the " spots of time " as it is from the experiences of the " spots of time " to the narrative matters. The distance is the same either way. Again it seems to me that a curious exploitation of the biographical substance of the work tends to postpone an appreciation of the poetry itself.

Thus far, then, we have remarked two important observations made by the poet: One, that often in *The Prelude* we are not treating matter of plain memory; the other, that in high and important passages of the poem the breath of the communicable fails and words faint weakly before they can touch the hidden truth. How far removed from problems of mere accuracy these statements leave us, and how distinctly they warn us of a certain critical irrelevance in dealing with *The Prelude* as something other than a poetic record of the growth of a poet's mind!

We may have anticipated that in matters of accuracy Wordsworth would fail in this poem, and that is precisely what he does. The fact that he does in no way impugns his poetic integrity; for, I think, and I have tried to suggest, that it has no authentic reference to that integrity.[3] The theme of the Fifth Book of *The Prelude* is Books. For some reason the poet is troubled over the open-

[3] In *The Prose Works of William Wordsworth*, Vol. III, ed by Rev. Alexander B. Grosart, we find among the Notes and Illustrations of the Poems some pertinent remarks by the poet. 1. *An Evening Walk* (p. 5): " The plan of it has not been confined to a particular walk, or an individual place; a proof of my unwillingness to submit the poetic spirit to the chains of fact and real circumstance. The country is idealized rather than described in any of its local aspects." 2. *The White Doe* (p. 124): " The poetry, if there be any in the work, proceeds, as it ought to do, from the *soul of man*, communicating its creative energies to the images of the external world." 3. *Suggested by a View* (p. 144): " The Hartshorn tree . . . though it was universally known to be a ' sycamore,' was always called the ' Round Thorn,' so difficult is it to chain fancy down to fact." Cf. the comment on " the little reflection with which even men of sense read poetry," (p. 283).

ing lines, leaving us as many as seven versions of them. The noble verses as we have them in the recension of 1850 deal with a concept, possibly announced by Kepler, of the explosion or fiery disintegration of the earth, and its gradual rehabilitation. But, muses the poet, when the earth is again able to foster life, alas, "The consecrated works of Bard and Sage" will be no more! We then come to a break in the poem, at verse 49, and must compare the 1805 version with that of 1850.

1805

One day, when in the hearing of a Friend,
I had given utterance to thoughts like these,
He answer'd with a smile that, in plain truth
'Twas going far to seek disquietude;
But on the front of his reproof, confess'd
That he, at sundry seasons, had himself
Yielded to kindred hauntings. And forthwith
Added, that once upon a summer's noon,
While he was sitting in a rocky cave, etc.

1850

One day, when from my lips a like complaint
Had fallen in presence of a studious friend,
He with a smile made answer, that in truth
'Twas going far to seek disquietude;
But on the front of his reproof confessed
That he himself had oftentimes given way
To kindred hauntings. Whereupon I told
That once in the stillness of a summer's noon,
While I was seated in a rocky cave, etc.

In either case there follows " a dream, which reaches the very *ne plus ultra* of sublimity, expressly framed to illustrate the eternity, and the independence of all social modes or fashions of existence, conceded to those two hemispheres, as it were, that compose the total world of human power—mathematics on the one hand, poetry on the other." [4] To this comment by De Quincey Ernest de Selincourt adds, in his Notes to *The Prelude*:

It will be noted that in all texts prior to the corrected D, i. e. 1839, Wordsworth gives this dream to his friend and not to himself. This is the more appropriate dramatically, for otherwise the friend has little reason for appearance in the poem at all; but it is far less probable.

[4] Thomas De Quincey, *Collected Works*, ed. by David Masson (London, 1896-7), ii. 268.

Wordsworth is not likely to have had a friend, however 'studious,' who could combine as Wordsworth did, a passion for the three threads of interest of which this dream is subtly interwoven—Cervantes, whom he read while still a schoolboy, tales of travel, and mathematics.[5]

What a magnificent privilege of probability de Selincourt has granted the poet!

Not being concerned, however, with whether Wordsworth or, let us say, Coleridge (who tramped to the *Valley of Rocks* with Hazlitt, where beneath precipices overhanging the sea there were rocky caverns) would the more probably fall asleep in an ocean cave at noon and dream " a dream, which reaches the very *ne plus ultra* of sublimity," it is my concern to point out that in the one instance " a dream, framed to illustrate the eternity, and the independence of all social modes or fashions of existence " is ascribed to the Friend, and in the other instance to the poet himself. In so far as the poetry of the passage is concerned, this discrepancy concerns me not at all. But such discrepancy must seriously concern the critic who ascribes significance to passages in *The Prelude* apart from the essential significance of the poetry itself. His concern might further be prompted by Harper's suggestion that the poem is not free from other forms of confusion.[6]

[5] *The Prelude* ed. by E. de Selincourt (Oxford, 1926), p. 526.

[6] There are, for instance, in' the 1805 and the 1850 versions curious variations in references to time. I give a few:

1805. I. 310-11: " ere I had seen Nine summers."
1850. I. 306-7: " ere I had told ten birthdays."
1805. VII. 1: " Five years are vanished since I first pour'd out."
1850. VII. 1: " Six changeful years have vanished since I first."
1805. VII. 12-13: " Not heard again until a little space
Before last primrose-time."
1850. VII. 11-12: " not audible again
Before last primrose-time."
1805. VII. 72-3: " 'Twas at least two years
Before this season when I first beheld."
1850. VII. 65-6: " Three years had flown
Since I had felt in heart and soul the shock."
1805. VII. 412: " It was but little more than three short years."
1850. VII. 382: " Four rapid years had scarcely then been told."
1805. VIII. 481-2: " not less
Than three and twenty summers had been told."
1850. VIII. 348-9: " not less
Than two and twenty summers had been told."
1805. X. 203: " (After a whole year's absence) I returned."
**1850. X. 236-7: " Twice had the trees let fall
Their leaves."**

In pointing out these problems in dealing with *The Prelude* it has not been my intention to belittle narrative matters or biographical data when they can be fairly ascertained and clearly evaluated. I have, of course, and for reasons which I hope are now patent, objected to informing the poem with biographical meaning and then informing ourselves with some supposed poetical meaning derived from the biographical. Since the poet confessedly has it as his presiding purpose often to deal with matters which lie beyond the call of plain memory, and with matters which " in the main lie far hidden from the reach of words "; and since he is uncertain or careless as to whether a great dream or vision was his or another's, I would suggest that students of the poem guard their speculations and distinguish between the critical values which may be drawn from factual data and those which may be derived from a contemplation of *The Prelude* as a poem designed to treat the growth of a poet's mind.

University of Michigan.

WORDSWORTH'S *PRELUDE:* THE POETIC
FUNCTION OF MEMORY

By Bennett Weaver

"Each man is a memory to himself."   III. 189.

I

When Andrew J. George wrote of "My Heart Leaps Up," "It
is *The Prelude* condensed into a lyric," he gave precise expression to
what became a common concept. As soon, however, as one attempts
to reverse the statement, one senses its inadequacy. The *Prelude*
is more than an expansion of the lyric. "Natural piety" is not
the withe which binds together the days of the greater poem. Nor
is it so much the continuity of being which the poet craves as an
instant unity. He must draw himself together tightly, so tightly
that time ceases to be consequential. Continuity carries the idea
of time in it; unity does not. It is the unity of being which the
poet seeks, it is that which he must have. The power which maintains for Wordsworth the necessitous unity is memory. This we
knew in the *Prelude* of 1850.

But the earlier version gives edge to our inquiry about the poetic
function of memory. We begin to suspect that when Wordsworth
speaks of this power of the mind he often means something distinct
and peculiar; and we have reason to believe that what he means by
memory in 1805, is at times vitally different from that which he
means in 1850. In 1805, memory is enhanced with witchery. It
visits the hiding-places of his power at will, and returns joyously.
But in the long interval between 1805 and the final revision, when
age *has* come on, Wordsworth "may scarcely see at all." The light
is often dim. What in 1805 he foresaw has in sad reality come
true. The record of fact corresponds to the language of prophecy.
And the point is simply that the poetic memory is a vital function
of the poetic mind, and that when the mind begins to fail the
function of memory is impaired. Wordsworth himself might say
that when the function of memory is lethargied, then the mind of
the poet fails. However the matter is put, it is worth investigation.

We may clarify our study by noticing the difference between a
poetically live use of the term in 1805, and a poetically dead use of
it in 1850. It would, of course, take more than a mathematical

quoting and counter-quoting of passages to go beyond mere illustration of the change which I suggest, and for the present I seek illustration only. We may, in the seventh book, read these lines:

> Attention comes,
> And comprehensiveness and memory,
> From early converse with the works of God
> Among all regions; chiefly where appear
> Most obviously simplicity and power.   VII. 716-720.

Memory aids in giving to the mind the grandeur of the mountain, in shaping for the soul an inner majesty. Here is the poetic implication that in memory the soul " retains an obscure sense of possible sublimity " (II. 334-337). The assumption of the Intimations Ode is already before us. The word, sharing the quality of the lines in which it appears, is replete with poetic suggestion.

In this same seventh book, however, we find Wordsworth using the word memory four times in 1850 in places where in 1805 he did not use it. Twice the term is smothered with narrative dullness, coming to nothing more than this:

> The mother now
> Is fading out of memory, but I see
> The lovely Boy as I beheld him then.   VII. 365-367.

Once the term is used in dead statement:

> Me, rather, it employed, to note, and keep
> In memory, those individual sights
> Of courage, or integrity, or truth.   VII. 598-600.

In the fourth instance I find that very poetical blankness which the man who wrote *To the Cuckoo* could not have tolerated. There is nothing which distinguishes between the metaphysical and the poetical, nothing which is blithe and golden, little that is blessed with an awareness of that spiritual condition in which the twofold voice of hope and love enraptures the soul. Wordsworth is capable of sounding on with philosophical terms long after all live thought has dried out of them. Although in the 1850 version he has strengthened many passages, ridding out surplusage, clarifying ideas and adding beauty to the manner of his lines, he sometimes practices desiccation. In 1805 the poet wrote these words:

> The matter that detains me now may seem,
> To many neither dignified enough

> Nor arduous; and is, doubtless, in itself
> Humble and low; yet not to be despis'd
> By those who have observ'd the curious props
> By which the perishable hours of life
> Rest on each other.   VII. 488-494.

This is not poetry, and Wordsworth knew it. Yet it is unified and
in the main sensible. When he attempted to make it into poetry
(1850) it is doubtful that he succeeded; since he destroyed the
unity and confused the sense.

> The matter that detains us now may seem
> To many, neither dignified enough
> Nor arduous, yet will not be scorned by them
> Who, looking inward, have observed the ties
> That bind the perishable hours of life
> Each to the other, and the curious props
> By which the world of memory and thought
> Exists and is sustained.   VII. 458-465.

Here the word memory hangs like an interdict upon the lines. It
partakes of the bad writing of the passage, and reads without
aesthetic definition.[1]

Perhaps it is sufficient to remark that Wordsworth was sensitive
to " the menace of the years." He knew that " the years of life
Were going on " (XI. 39-40), that the " Poetic spirit " is in " after
years abated and suppressed " (II. 276) ; that the " weight of life "
causes the brightest rapture to flee away (V. 569); that " the
morning gladness " is indeed of the morning alone (VI. 63) ; and
that vision fails (XI. 339). It is for this very reason that memory
plays so important a part in the building up, the saving, and the
restoring of his mind. It is for this reason, also, that memory itself
associates with the other grand faculties of the mind, with fancy
and imagination, with sense and thought, living while they live,
failing when they fail. And this being true, it follows that there is
point to our study of the restorative and unifying faculty of the
poet's mind in the days when languor was for him a phase of
" redundant energy," and not a spreading weakness that sicklied
o'er the paling casts of his passion.

---

[1] It is interesting to note that in almost all of the thirteen passages in
which the term memory is used in the poetically drowsy *Excursion*, we
find this lack of aesthetic quality. See 1. 391; 3. 400, 431, 574, 847;
4. 997; 5. 48; 6. 253, 702, 1082; 7. 29, 388, 999.

II

When Keats wished to characterize Wordsworth's poetical genius as distinguished from his own, he recognized that what marked the older man was a continuous sinking deep and rising high within himself, a characteristic that he acutely called the "egotistical Sublime; which is a thing per se, and stands alone" (To Richard Woodhouse, Oct. 27, 1818). Keats wrote the truth. Aloneness is the boast of Wordsworth's soul: "A mind forever voyaging through strange seas of thought alone." For Wordsworth the holiest place he knows is his own soul (X. 381). That, after all, is the proper haunt of his genius. It is for this reason and it is in response to an infallible artistic compulsion that he turns "the mind in upon itself" (III. 112), pores, watches, expects, listens. It is for this reason that he spreads his thoughts wide and wider until he feels

> Incumbencies more awful, visitings
> Of the Upholder of the tranquil Soul.   III. 115-116.

By this means he ascends to "community with highest truth" (III. 120). *What* happens to this mind is vital to it, and *how* it happens is of almost imponderable importance. The faculty which in this mind can restore the *what* and recall the *how,* or exalt the mind with shadowy suggestions of sublimity, is a faculty far different from that which ordinarily we call memory.

It is patent that we are investigating no mere factual memory, memory of the basket kind which holds in its dead weave whatever is tossed into it. We study a living power, an agency of creative genius. From the reach of all words whose use is in their exactitude this power may "lie far hidden." But it is through it that the *Prelude* gains its marvelous substantiality. It is through it that we are made more clearly aware of the other powers of the poet's mind and their sympathetic and cooperative activity.

There is in the fourth book (1805) a carefully detailed metaphor of the mind, with memory now like fancy, memory whose substances cannot certainly be distinguished from the shadows of fancy. The poet has been recalling incidents of his summer vacation and the feelings associated with them.

> As one who hangs down-bending from the side
> Of a slow-moving Boat, upon the breast
> Of a still water, solacing himself

> With such discoveries as his eye can make,
> Beneath him, in the bottom of the deeps,
> Sees many beauteous sights, weeds, fishes, flowers,
> Grots, pebbles, roots of trees, and fancies more;
> Yet often is perplex'd, and cannot part
> The shadow from the substance, rocks and sky,
> Mountains and clouds, from that which is indeed
> The region, and the things which there abide
> In their true dwelling; now is cross'd by gleam
> Of his own image, by a sunbeam now,
> And motions that are sent he knows not whence,
> Impediments that make his task more sweet;
> —Such pleasant office have we long pursued
> Incumbent o'er the surface of past time.   IV. 247-263.

This passage is more than an apologetic explanation of the confusions which assail ordinary memory. It is a trope, poetical in itself, suggesting higher truth about poetic memory. It does confess, and it is an important confession, that the poet is unable to distinguish between the real and the unreal in the depths of his mind,—a truth that should make us forever hesitant about attempting to set historical facts upon the liquid surfaces of poetry. But, for the moment, the pertinent thing about the passage is that it reveals the vital nature of poetic memory. It is a working thing which sees and fancies and delights in its own ways. It is aware of indeterminate impulses and it celebrates the union of shadow and substance. Of this union it knows poetry is born. Nothing characterizes prose so much as its factual affinities; and nothing characterizes poetry more than its affinity for truth. Memory, then, in the poet must work not with fact alone, but with that which is born living from fact and fancy. The poet's business is other than the prose writer's: his business is with poetic truth. Wordsworth himself, in his *Essay, Supplementary to the Preface,* has pronounced upon the matter: " The appropriate business of poetry (which, nevertheless, if genuine, is as permanent as pure science), her appropriate employment, her privilege and her *duty,* is to treat of things not as they *are,* but as they *appear*; not as they exist in themselves, but as they *seem* to exist to the senses, and to the *passions.*"

The poet, then, would give up his integrity and the proper understanding of himself if he dealt with the past as fixed or dead actuality. He must treat the past after his true nature, letting his living mind proceed creatively into the past and not allowing the dead past to come into his mind with all its unnatural prerogatives. Wordsworth is too shrewd to presume for a moment that anything other can be the case with the artist. It is the one who does not reflect upon the true nature of the mind who does not see that each possible fact is a dead, disconnected, and essentially unknowable thing; that it can take on being and significance only when the mind gives it meaning; and that the process of giving meaning to bygone facts is just the process of recollection which Wordsworth described. In other words, through the nature of poetic memory, the vitality of the mind assimilates all into the mind; and the poetry which results is of another truth than the truth of tabulation.

When, therefore, Wordsworth writes " the history of a poet's mind," he writes essentially in terms of this other truth. This is not to impugn the soundness of certain data in the poem, but rather to keep from confusing whatever of mere biography there is in it with whatever there is of pure poetry. Even in the seventh book, which is characterized by astonishing masses of data, data which in some cases are surely not assimilated into poetry, we find these lines in the 1805 version:

> Shall I give way
> Copying the impression of the memory,
> Though things unnumber'd idly do half seem
> The work of fancy? VII. 145-148.

And the answer is, " Yes, for pastime's sake, I shall. These are day-dreams where colours, lights, and forms change curiously. It will not be unamusing to play with them." We lose this passage and something of its fine and careless candor in the later version. But we need not lose the point.

As he closes his comment upon his life at Cambridge, Wordsworth makes a statement replete with high honesty, frank, and full of truth. By doing so he surely does not intend to discredit the revelations of the third book. The distinction which he seems to pass against " naked recollection " as compared with " after-meditation," is a distinction he would have us make, not curiously, but generously. He would have us know that a prose record of the growth of a poet's mind would be at last an impossible anomaly, and that only in poetry can be recorded finally the experiences which have entered into that growth.

> Of these and other kindred notices
> I cannot say what portion is in truth
> The naked recollection of that time,
> And what may rather have been call'd to life
> By after-meditation.   III. 644-648.

These lines are momentous and through them we must deepen our study. As we have found the poet lightly but significantly confessing the relationship between fancy and memory, so here we find him posing naked recollection over against after-meditation, and stating that he cannot in truth tell what portion of the experiences which he attributes to his days at Cambridge belongs to the one or to the other. I repeat, this matter is worthy of our closest attention. In the term after-meditation, we recognize a quality peculiarly Wordsworthian. The word itself, in short, is one of the most confessional words of the entire poem; and if we pause to sense its full meaning we shall find it of a piece with the poet's theory of poetic composition. This characteristic meditating upon the past calls into life and being—what? Perchance what never actually happened at Cambridge, or in any other earthly place. For the mind may make her notices for herself, and give them timeless being. What, then, is poetic memory? What is truth? We follow the poet's way.

Fancy and memory, naked recollection and after-mediation,—we are coming closer to the vital center of this poet's mind. I say vital center, not only because the higher memory is at various times between 1795 and 1805 recognized as a living quality of the mind, but also because near the beginning of his poem Wordsworth has made it clear that it is no less than to fix the wavering balance of his mind that he has set out to fetch

> Invigorating thoughts from former years.   I. 649.

If he is to help his friend understand how his heart was framed, and if he is to gain poise and strength for his task, then he must make clear not only to his friend, but also to himself the " goings-on " of this power which we study. Pushing his way through paradox after paradox, he writes:

> Need I dread from thee
> Harsh judgments, if I am so loth to quit
> Those recollected hours that have the charm
> Of visionary things, and lovely forms
> And sweet sensations that throw back our life
> And *almost* make our Infancy itself
> A visible scene, on which the sun is shining?   I. 653-663.

Here the process of recollection begins to associate itself with the purely visionary. After-meditation leads into abstraction, and abstraction reaches beyond fancy and forward from fancy into scenes made right for the mind's joy. The process of recollection moves with sweet stealthiness, putting on the charm of dream. It is because of this charm that the poet, whose inner mind had so much of weary darkness in it, is granted an awareness of the scene of infancy " on which the sun is shining." This bright apprehension gives the poet new hope and vigor. And when he reworks the lines for the 1850 edition, in order to deepen the insistence of them, he changes " infancy itself " to " remotest infancy." It is no vulgar power of recollection which we see here, but a power grown imperial.

This imperious zest for the past which is touched by the charm of the visionary, drives the mind of the poet back and back, until memory becomes transmuted into that poetic faith which pitches full into the Infinite. But first Wordsworth must gain the sun-flashing scene of Infancy itself. It cannot be by chance that he repeats the word *almost* in two passages dealing with this matter, since those passages are as far apart as the first and the eleventh books, and since both were carefully worked over for the later version, the word remaining untouched. The first passage has in it also that gleam of light which memory grown meditative pleases to cast upon early scenes.

> Unfading recollections! at this hour
> The heart is *almost* mine with which I felt
> From some hill-top, on sunny afternoons
> The Kite high up among the fleecy clouds
> Pull at its rein.   I. 517-521.

We may, in a passage so lightly philosophical, sense too keenly the assertive accent of " Unfading recollection," while our main objective is to observe that through feeling the poet recalls what he fancies he felt.

As we come into the selection from the later book, however, we find ourselves dealing with matter of more import. Memory becomes the substance of things unseen.

> Oh! mystery of Man, from what a depth
> Proceed thy honours! I am lost, but see
> In simple childhood something of the base
> On which thy greatness stands . . .

> The days gone by
> Come back upon me from the dawn *almost*
> Of life: the hiding-places of my power
> Seem open; I approach, and then they close;
> I see by glimpses now; when age comes on,
> May scarcely see at all, and I would give,
> While yet we may, as far as words can give,
> A substance and a life to what I feel:
> I would enshrine the spirit of the past
> For future restoration.   XI. 329-343.

This is a strange result to come from the " visionary dreariness " felt by a child five and one-half years old and the pleasure felt by a youth " in the blessed time of early love,"—but " So," the poet assures us, " feeling comes in aid Of feeling " (XI. 326). It is through feeling that memory strives to " enshrine the spirit of the past "; and we observe that this living power has taken the poet back *almost* to the dawn of life, *almost* to the hiding-places of his power, *almost* to the source of his poetic being.

We can, I think, in these three passages feel Wordsworth wishing to put this word *almost* into his pocket and say no more about it. Obviously, he is too honest to do this; obviously, he wishes he might do it in order to range with perfect freedom those long prospects of the mind which lead into infinity. His " unwillingness to submit the poetic spirit to the chains of fact and real circumstance," works subtly in him. He precipitates his confusion into a paradox, letting his poetic need master him. In short, he tells us that he has been writing both of emotions and of " unremembered " things, " things silently gone out of mind " (Preface, 1802); things that have wearied themselves out of the memory (I. 626); or things that have been disowned by it (I. 643).

> I began
> My story early, feeling as I fear
> The weakness of a human love, for days
> Disown'd by memory, ere the birth of spring
> Planting my snowdrops among winter snows!   I. 640-644.

The " birth of spring," or " breath of spring," as he refers to it in the 1850 recension, would be the time of the beginning of actual memory in his mind; the " winter snows " would be associated with the time before the beginning of actual memory; and the " snowdrops " would be the things that grow out of after-meditation and " human love, for days Disown'd by memory." They are not of the actual memory at all; they are of the preceding poetic memory. As things created by the working imagination are to things merely perceived, so are these snowdrops to all that the mind might remember in flat and factual ways. If we watch shrewdly and remember always that we are reading poetry about the growth of a poetic mind, we shall understand why Wordsworth " took hold of the notion of pre-existence," using it as a machine to move " the world of his own mind." The thought of Plato was for him a mere convenience in explanation; the comprehension of the higher reaches of poetic memory was his own. It is " the world of his own mind " with which we should concern ourselves.

The paradox implied in speaking of " things silently gone out of mind " and in dealing with things forgotten at the very birth of our earthly being, is in part resolved by Wordsworth's association of memory with feeling. He may in this be in some manner under the influence of Hartleian sensism,[2] although how much it were wrong positively to assert. Where the thinking of one man falls into the natural need of another, it is wise to turn from analyzing the food to understand the hunger. There are always two ends to every influence, although the scholar has busied himself largely with the dead end. The theory of Hartley implies among other things that whatever has entered the mind through the senses cannot pass from the mind. No assumption could more generously satisfy Wordsworth's need of reaching back to the sources of his existence. I have no doubt that the need in him would have forced its own satisfaction, Hartley or no. He was walking strongly in that direction, and I think in that direction he would have gone. If he came upon a path prepared, and took it, that is one matter. Under other circumstances he would probably have arrived at the same place.

There seem to be two phases to sense-memory: one in which the " vulgar joy by its own weight wearies itself out of the memory," although " The scenes which were a witness of that joy " (I. 626-627) remain; the other in which " obscure feelings " are " representative of joys (things, 1850) that were forgotten " (I. 634-635), and ally " these same scenes " to the affections. In the first case the passion of the sounding cataract would have wearied itself away,

---

[2] Here it may be to the point to recall the " feelings Of unremembered pleasure," the " unremembered acts ": *Tintern Abbey.*

although the waterfall itself would have remained in its " substantial lineaments Depicted on the brain " (I. 628-629) ; in the second case " obscure feelings " would have come to represent the passion which had wearied itself away. This second phase is far more subtle and tenuous than the first, and undoubtedly becomes the means by which, in an *a posteriori* manner, reasoning from effect to cause, Wordsworth ultimately justifies his speaking of unremembered things. For the feeling represents the thing, and could not have been unless the thing once existed. Hence, in the exalted ways of poetic reasoning, the feeling postulates the something " silently gone out of mind."

> The soul,
> Remembering *how* she felt, but *what* she felt
> Remembering not, retains an obscure sense
> Of possible sublimity.   II. 334-337.

Memory here seems none other than an exalted process of feeling. She has doubly transcended the factual, and has come into her high poetic service. Nothing can gainsay her intimations; and whereas in the first book we have " obscure feelings representative Of joys that were forgotten," we now have " an obscure sense Of possible sublimity." It is union with the sublime which was the recurrent and imperious need of the fully empowered poet, and it is at last through the poetically sublimated memory that he satisfies the need. Not only must he be within himself an instant unit, but also must he be unified with the Eternal Sublimity. So memory comes " From early converse with the works of God " (VII. 716-718). She releases " what she felt " ; for its precious assurance she retains " how she felt." She lives in continually recreating herself within the Created. Through her the poet's mind grows whole.

III

Since Wordsworth's need of this mystical wholeness was so thorough and so acute during his great decade, we may conclude that the higher memory is one of the master keys to his mind. By observing what he said of feelings representative of joys forgotten and of the soul's remembering how she felt, we may read with fresh understanding what he tells us of his method of composing poetry.

I have said that poetry is the spontaneous overflow of powerful feelings: it takes its origin from emotion recollected in tranquility; the emotion is contemplated till, by a species of re-action, the tranquility gradually disappears, and an emotion, kindred to that which was before the subject of contemplation, is gradually produced, and does actually exist in the mind.

This is an explanation of Wordsworth's peculiar power. Before he composes he gathers himself together where he is to work. He is sure of his truth. The new emotion, not in fact spontaneously but gradually derived from the former emotion, has in it the integrity of the then and now. The poet becomes a whole man. Feeling comes in aid of feeling, thought comes in aid of thought, and feeling and thought come in aid of each other until the poet is assured that, having achieved a perfect integrity, he may speak his truth, and his truth will be the truth for all men.

University of Michigan.

WORDSWORTH: FORMS AND IMAGES

By Bennett Weaver

I

> The visible scene
> Would enter unawares into his mind
> With all its solemn imagery, its rocks,
> Its woods, and that uncertain heaven received
> Into the bosom of the steady lake.
>
> *The Prelude* V. 409-413.

In these words Mr. Garrod [1] finds the " starting point, the well-head of all " Wordsworth's thinking. The scholar does not, unfortunately, allow himself to treat fully the meaning of his statement; but that his remark strikes to the white of truth there can be little doubt. The depth of his penetration is revealed when he says that the experience referred to in the verses " may be called a perfectly familiar experience. Each one of us can call to mind in his own recollections, analogues to it. It may be called perfectly ordinary." It may be, in other words, an experience which men unread in the philosophers and uninfluenced by them can have. I want to begin with this fair and sane assumption, hoping that by such an approach we may come into a fuller understanding of the poet's mind.

There is, in fact, an unremarked naturalness in what Wordsworth tells us of the experiences which his mind had with the forms and images of nature. The grand comment which he makes—and, in its way, also, " it may be called perfectly ordinary "—is that at first he reacted in a sensuous way to the physical qualities of these things, and that later he reacted in a spiritual way to the " eternal Beauty," the source of these things. We shall scrutinize the minute modifications which should be made of this statement, but we shall not find it basically qualified. And always when we have found within the experience and the mind of the poet a sufficient cause we shall not go beyond that cause to consider influences which in the nature of the case must be infected with irrelevance. Even when we find in the poet the very words of another, or the echoes of another's tongue, we shall remember that these words and echoes

---

[1] Heathcote William Garrod, *Wordsworth: Lectures and Essays* (Oxford, 1927), p. 96.

cannot prove that the poetic ideas under treatment came from any source other than the poet's mind. All of us have been delighted with finding our own ideas expressed in the words of another; and when the words are attractive to us we naturally use them to utter our own ideas. In this way Shakespeare has been of service to myriads of men, and our delight in him often arises from his anticipatory understanding of us. He does not so much influence us as express us. If, then, in the past we have profited by coming to the mind of Wordsworth through the minds of other men, it would now seem that we might supplement this practice by a more sufficient directness.

In the *Prelude* of 1805, there are at least eight passages which treat Wordsworth's basic experience with the forms and images of nature. In these passages he repeatedly tells us of some visible form's entering his mind, exciting in him an immediate, extrinsic, and organic joy. Although this joy later be subtilized and sublimated to "intercourse with the eternal Beauty," although the physical delight become spiritual ecstasy, there is at first a pleasure sheer and instant. It is such pleasure as in our degree we all have known in the lines of trees, in the flowing shapes of clouds, in the undulation of a meadow moving low among the hills, and in the forms of the hills themselves. Wordsworth had an eye for all these things, and how clearly he saw and how well he understood what he saw, his *Guide to the Lakes* makes known.

The idea of "pure organic pleasure" in forms extrinsic to the mind was with the poet early in life. When, in his "Lines composed a few miles above Tintern Abbey," Wordsworth wishes to suggest the intensity, the immediacy of his reaction to the colors and forms of Nature, he describes that reaction as "an appetite." He shades his thought awkwardly, honestly, building out the element which characterized his feeling for the rocks and cataracts with the suggestion of coarseness, or animal quality. For him, and for us alike, there is no word capable of expressing perfectly the "delicate, snailhorn perception" of that instant when within the eye form is purely form, and when within the heart of man his joy in pure form is pure. Wordsworth suggests these things almost as well as one may, at least with a clarity sufficient to make it known that he is aware of them. Yet it is to be remarked that in these same "Lines" the poet ascribes a profound experience of his mind to the influence of " beauteous forms " upon it. Through their magic powers they have so wrought in him that he, " laid asleep in body, and become a living soul," sees " into the life of things." So we have in this one poem a suggestion of the beginning and end of the matter, the one implied in the other, and both, to use the acute expression of Mr. Garrod, " perfectly ordinary."

The probability that the first and second books of the *Prelude* were completed before 1800, leads one to anticipate in these books certain thoughts similar to those of the " Lines." How similar the thought regarding forms may be is suggested by the following passage.

> Yes, I remember, when the changeful earth,
> And twice five seasons on my mind had stamp'd
> The faces of the moving year, even then,
> A Child, I held unconscious intercourse
> With the eternal Beauty, drinking in
> A pure organic pleasure from the lines
> Of curling mists, or from the level plain
> Of waters colour'd by the steady clouds.
>
> I. 586-593.

In understanding the significance of these lines we are curiously aided by the very passage to which Mr. Garrod made reference,[2] that one describing the boy known by the " Islands of Winander." This passage, although placed in book five, which was not written until after the spring of 1804, was itself composed in Germany at least four years earlier. Not at all strangely, it is about another boy named William, and I make no doubt that it was the name William that the poet gazed upon abstractedly, as he stood in the Churchyard " above the Village School." Whereas William Wordsworth, in the lines which we have quoted, is " twice five seasons " old, William Raincock is on this side of " full ten years." The " changeful earth " of the one is the " visible scene " of the other, and where " The faces of the moving year " stamp themselves upon the mind of the one William, " the visible scene With all its solemn imagery " enters the mind of the other unawares. It is small wonder that William the poet often stood " A long half-hour together . . . Mute—looking at the grave in which " William of Rayrigg lay; for he was engaged in his most haunting contemplation, that of his own mind. Again, although in another way, we come near " the well-head " of all his thinking.

[2] *Loc. cit.*

However, the lines in the first book go beyond those in the fifth. For both passages the *locus* is the same: in the one, we gaze upon " the level plain of waters colour'd by the steady clouds "; in the other, we look " Into the bosom of the steady Lake." Yet in the first book, Wordsworth has not written clearly and, if one may trust his later attempts to change the lines, he did not express exactly what he meant to say. To drink in " organic pleasure " from " the eternal Beauty " would be a base and impossible thing. In the place of " the eternal Beauty," he later writes, " old as creation." By 1850, he has worked over the three final verses, expunging one word which I regard as significant. That word is *lines*, for which he substitutes the pretty, verse-filling " silver wreaths." So, also, in his reference to the clouds, he changes the just word *steady* for the poetically dull word *impending*. I mean especially to point out that the " organic pleasure," relieved of its confusion with " the eternal Beauty," seems to be derived from the lines of the mist and the colored forms of the clouds as they are reflected in the water. The sharp sensitiveness to lines and the full reaction to colored forms which mark these verses, are to be noted, but it is also to be remembered that there is nothing about this sensitiveness not implicit in the poetic mind.

In the transition from the " pure organic pleasure " in the lines and colors of objects, to a spiritual joy in the " Wisdom of the Universe," the poet passes through the sweet purgations of early maturity. The extrinsic form must become the intrinsic quality. The steadiness and grandeur of the " mountain's outline " must be transmuted into a steadiness and grandeur of the soul. When, in the individual, this process is aided by " a peculiar sensibility of original organization " it will go on swiftly and deeply. Yet so irresistible is the power within the process that it sweeps through general as well as peculiar sensibility, affecting whole peoples. " Natural objects " are effective " in forming the character of Nations. . . . All are more or less affected by them." The beauty in form becomes the beauty in the mind; and after the mind has become spiritualized by the transmutation, then it can hold direct converse with the " Spirit of the Universe." Man, so quickened, " Shall hear far Chaos talk with " him. Wordsworth, at other times, shall find a swifter way to this consummation; but for the present

By influence habitual to the mind
The mountain's outline and its steady form
Gives a pure grandeur, and its presence shapes
The measure and the prospect of the soul
To majesty; such virtue have the forms
Perennial of the ancient hills. . . .
The Soul of Beauty and enduring life
Was present as a habit, and diffused,
Through meagre lines and colours, and the press
Of self-destroying, transitory things
Composure and ennobling harmony.

VII. 721-740.

Once the mind has been given " a pure grandeur " by the " mountain's outline," and once the " prospect of the soul " has been shaped " to majesty," then the soul is in a measure prepared for intercourse with the " eternal Beauty." Deep speaks unto deep and power is changed with power. " Think," cries the poet, " the Wisdom and Spirit of the universe, the Presence whose dwelling is the light of setting suns, gives everlasting motion to forms and images! With these forms and images the Presence intertwines the passions of my mind, purifying, sanctifying, disciplining me until I am aware of the grandeur in the beating of my heart " (I. 428-441).

II

There is, however, beyond the ennobling of the heart another distinct service which forms render the poet. They become the substances and solidities with which the creative power works. This function of form is of profound importance. For the temptation of the poet is to " pipe Among the Shepherds," to let the fancy roam, to deal with airy nothingness, to luxuriate in the fantastic, to seek the soft involvements of artificial raptures. Not without severe discipline does he treat of " the passions of men incorporated with the beautiful and permanent forms of nature." And one who passes the bands of choiring angels does not come back easily to prettiness. It is in forms that Wordsworth finds a substantial power not only arresting him from wild vagaries, but also releasing him to noble creation.

Forms and images, then, are aids to his high toil. It is not his to tread " The hemisphere of magic fiction." No one in his youth could have had " more bright appearances " of the fairy world; but

2

there is in him an " inner knowledge " of such depth that he dares
not roam the gorgeous fields of fantasy. His " home is with infinitude "; and in that home all is ordered, nothing phantasmic. The
exuberant fictive power which trifles with Nature, rendering the
ghostly ghastly, and the " tragic supertragic," and not able to rest
until it has strained all and distorted and stretched it into flaccidity,
has no place in the ordered world of art. It is an " adulterate
Power."

> Yet in the midst
> Of these vagaries, with an eye so rich
> As mine was, through the chance, on me not wasted
> Of having been brought up in such a grand
> And lovely region, I had forms distinct
> To steady me; . . .
> At all times had a real solid world
> Of images about me.
>
> VIII. 593-604.

Even as these forms of " a real solid world " protected him from
the " adulterate Power " of " wilful fancy," so fancy herself, once
purified and steadied by judgment, might aid the poet.

> Then might we return
> And in the Rivers and the Groves behold
> Another face, might hear them from all sides
> Calling upon the more instructed mind
> To link their images with subtle skill
> Sometimes, and by elaborate research
> With forms and definite appearances
> Of human life, presenting them sometimes
> To the involuntary sympathy
> Of our internal being.
>
> XIII. 294-303.

If fancy, straitened to her slight creative task, could utilize the
images of nature, and being steadied with them, could work for
man's delight, what might not the grand imagination do with all
that manifested the loveliness of the world? Wordsworth gives
to forms and images a peculiar functional importance.

III

Since we find forms to be the very elements with which Imagination works, except in moments transcendent with ecstasy, it is
natural that our study of them should help us to understand Words-

worth's antipathy for the "simple Reason," the lesser reason, the meddlesome intellect. For Imagination is "reason in her most exalted mood"; the "grand Reason" is an "awful Power" rising "from the mind's abyss,"—it is that, in short, which comes from the "blind cavern," or source of being, a synthesizing power, drawing all things into harmonious relationship with each other and with itself. It is this relationship, so uninteresting to Goethe, so necessary to Wordsworth, which the analytic reason destroys; and it destroys it by working among the forms and images of the visible universe to compare them in ways superficial, or to combine them in ways arbitrary which together numb the "inner faculties." It impairs Imagination. Confusedly the poet protests his innocence of this sin, and then confesses:

> Oh! Soul of Nature! that dost overflow
> With passion and with life, what feeble men
> Walk on this earth! how feeble have I been
> When thou wert in thy strength! Nor this through stroke
> Of human suffering, such as justifies
> Remissness and inaptitude of mind,
> But through presumption, even in pleasure pleas'd
> Unworthily, disliking here, and there,
> Liking, by rules of mimic art transferr'd
> To things above all art. But more, for this,
> Although a strong infection of the age,
> Was never much my habit, giving way
> To a comparison of scene with scene,
> Bent overmuch on superficial things,
> Pampering myself with meagre novelties
> Of colour and proportion, to the moods
> Of time and season, to the moral power
> The affections, and the spirit of the place,
> Less sensible.
>
> XI. 146-164.

This is neither outspoken nor clear. But he goes on, struggling toward the truth.

> Here only let me add that my delights,
> Such as they were, were sought insatiably,
> Though 'twas a transport of the outward sense,
> Not of the mind, vivid but not profound:
> Yet was I often greedy in the chace,
> And roam'd from hill to hill, from rock to rock,
> Still craving combinations of new forms,

> New pleasure, wider empire for the sight,
> Proud of its own endowments, and rejoiced
> To lay the inner faculties asleep.
>
> XI. 186-195.

Forms and new forms in their combinations, form throwing the
" outward sense " into transport, vivid and alluring forms, as barren to the poet as a siren to a sailor, with these the " simple Reason "
may not be trusted.   These are neither trifles for the toying of
Fancy nor creatures for the satiating of the sense; but they must be
brought to experience the deep fecundity of the Imagination. They
must be filled with meaning, relationship, and truth.

It was during the days between his leaving France in 1792, and
his settling at Racedown in 1795, that Wordsworth delivered himself
most closely polled and shaven to the intellect.   The cogency of the
syllogism gave a false security to his mind.   The charm of logic,
lifted over him by the grey witch-doctor Godwin, while seeming to
cure him, blackened his already " blind thoughts."   His life was
sick with " fears and fancies," and he was persuaded to cure himself
by sipping from the poison vials of his sickness.   " By logic and
minute analysis," so naturally pleasant to the growing mind, he
turned against that which he thought was false instead of toward
that which he knew to be true; and so become lost and wandered
miserably away from the centers of his comfort.   He no longer
could draw a dewy joy from

> Earth with all her appanage
> Of elements and organs, storm and sunshine,
> With its pure forms and colours, pomp of clouds
> Rivers and mountains.
>
> XI. 108-111.

Embosomed among these things, his instinct was to worship and to
make himself whole; but he was for the time given to " barren
intermeddling subtleties," and he suffered from the " strong infec-
tion of the age."   He lived under a tyranny false to him, and a
tyranny the more bitter because, with his own hands, he had affixed
his name to the bond that bound him to it.   He, too, " murdered
to dissect "; he, too, broke the forms of Nature apart from each
other and crushed them into rubble with which the analytic genius
could build nothing.   He allowed his lesser reason to make the whole
of him a chaos.   Aesthetic hypochondria was the substantial result.
His need was for the mystic simples of his youth,

> To drink wild water, and to pluck green herbs,
> And gather fruits fresh from their native bough.
>
> I. 37-38.

And there was one to nurse him, one whose mind had been " a mansion for all lovely forms." She opened up his inner eyes to loveliness again. Smiles broke from him and he had ease. Wordsworth became again a poet.

IV

In *The Recluse* of 1798, Wordsworth sought to chant the " spousal verse " of the wedding of the mind of men to " the external World," and of " external World " to the mind of man. Four years later, in his *Preface*, he defines poetry as " the image of men and nature "; and in answer to the question, " What then does the Poet? " he replies: " He considers man and the objects that surround him as acting and re-acting upon each other, so as to produce an infinite complexity of pain and pleasure. . . . He considers man and nature as essentially adapted to each other, and the mind of man as naturally the mirror of the fairest and most interesting properties of nature." And all of this sounds heavy with Hartley, with sensism and associationism. Were Wordsworth in the habit of being unconfused and single-minded, it would give us pause indeed. But here Mr. Rader [3] and Mr. Rea,[4] both sound and excellent students, help us, the one making it clear that the poet was not utterly under the dominance of Hartley, in 1802, and the other making it clear that the " brother of his soul," Coleridge, who is thought by some critics to have bent him toward Hartley, was at this time far in gestation by Proclus. Yet had these scholars by their research not made us safe in these conclusions, there is evidence within the *Recluse* itself, and within the *Preface*, which would justify us in drawing them. For, as we have seen, in the poem Wordsworth is explicit in referring to the " Mind of Man " as the " haunt, and main region " of his song; and he continues—

> Beauty—a living Presence of the earth
> Surpassing the most fair ideal Forms

---

[3] Melvin M. Rader, *Presiding Ideas in Wordsworth's Poetry* (University of Washington Press, 1931).

[4] John D. Rea, " Coleridge's Intimations of Immortality from Proclus," *MP*, XXVI (1928), 201.

Which craft of delicate Spirits hath composed
From earth's materials. . . .

The Recluse. 795-798.

Here manifestly the poet's mind is beginning to feel beyond forms for pure exaltation unprofaned by forms. Nothing characterizes this man more than his bent to subdue everything to the quality of his own mind. He may have tried to think that the informing of the mind through the senses, and the senses through the mind, were processes mutual and reciprocal, but his true genius was for the latter only. "What is a Poet?" Let us quote again from the *Preface,* willfully seeking the salvation of our argument: "He is a man who rejoices more than other men in the spirit of life that is in him; delighting to contemplate similar volitions and passions as manifested in the goings-on of the Universe, and habitually impelled to create them where he does not find them. To these qualities he has added a disposition to be affected more than other men by absent things as if they were present; an ability of conjuring up in himself passions, which are indeed far from being the same as those produced by real events; . . . a greater readiness and power in expressing what he thinks and feels, and especially those thoughts and feelings which, by his own choice, or from the structure of his own mind, arise in him without immediate external excitement." We have, in short, come to breathe the "breath and finer spirit of all knowledge," to observe the high creations which take place through form and beyond form.

Wordsworth early had warning that he must accustom himself to exist without the assurance of physical substantiality. Familiar as it is, we must quote again the Fenwick note:

I was often unable to think of external things as having external existence, and I communed with all that I saw as something not apart from but inherent in, my own immaterial nature. Many times while going to school have I grasped at a wall or tree to recall myself from this abyss of idealism to reality. At that time I was afraid of such processes. In later periods of life I have deplored, as we all have reason to, a subjugation of an opposite character, and have rejoiced over the remembrance, as is expressed in the lines "Obstinate questionings etc."

It was none other than this same process of becoming a living and poetic soul which he describes so remarkably in the first book of the *Prelude.* After he had, by "an act of stealth," taken the Shepherd's boat, he was severely disciplined by fear.

> For many days, my brain
> Work'd with a dim and undetermin'd sense
> Of unknown modes of being; in my thoughts
> There was a darkness, call it solitude,
> Or blank desertion, no familiar shapes
> Of hourly objects, images of trees,
> Of sea or sky, no colours of green fields;
> But huge and mighty Forms that do not live
> Like living men mov'd slowly through the mind
> By day and were the trouble of my dreams.
>
> I. 418-427.

It is through such experiences that he enters ever and again his own world, the visionary world " by form Or image unprofaned." " From unknown causes " the waters of his being are troubled, showing the efficacious angel near, although at such holy times the poet feels " left alone, Seeking the visible world, nor knowing why." The props of his affections are removed, and yet the building stands " as if sustained By its own spirit ! " This is to him matter of ecstatic amazement, suggesting the world beyond this world, the life beyond this life. For though haunted at first by these fallings from him, vanishings, he comes to recognize in them the fountain-light of all his day, the master-light of all his seeing. Just beyond the experience of finding

> Impress'd upon all forms the characters
> Of danger and desire
>
> I. 497-498.

lies the mighty Sinaic experience, though the mountain for Wordsworth be Snowdon.

It is only among the geometric forms of " pure Intelligence " that the poet finds those " pure proportions " which image the mind of the Divine Reality. Here in mathematics is the " solid evidence " of truth, truth that exalts the mind above uncertainty, dissolving contrarieties into harmony. Back of the form is the pure idea. To contemplate the pure idea brings " Transcendent peace And silence."

> Mighty is the charm
> Of those abstractions to a mind beset
> With images, and haunted by itself;
> And specially delightful unto me
> Was that clear Synthesis built up aloft
> So gracefully, . . .

an independent world
Created out of pure Intelligence.

VI. 178-187.

There is at last escape from the dominance of outward forms.
In his friend Coleridge, Wordsworth had observed a peculiar and
characteristic freedom from this dominance. The younger man, in
his *Table Talk,* had remarked that " a visit to the battle-field of
Marathon would raise in him no kindling emotion." Wordsworth
explained the statement by saying that " Coleridge was not under
the influence of external objects. He had extraordinary powers of
summoning up an image or series of images in his own mind, and
he might mean that his idea of Marathon was so vivid, that no
visible observation could make it more so. A remarkable instance
of this is his poem, said to be ' composed in the Vale of Chamouni.'
Now he never was at Chamouni, or near it, in his life." And Wordsworth might have added out of his own experience

> Be Chamouni unseen, unknown!
> It must, or we shall rue it:
> We have a vision of our own:
> And why should we undo it?

In other words, Coleridge, his " Twin almost in genius and in
mind," had his own power to scoop out " By help of dreams " what
he would. The comment in book seven of the *Prelude* is too similar
to evade.

> I have thought
> Of Thee, thy learning, gorgeous eloquence
> And all the strength and plumage of thy Youth,
> Thy subtle speculations, toils abstruse
> Among the Schoolmen, and platonic forms
> Of wild ideal pageantry, shap'd out
> From things well-match'd, or ill, and words for things,
> The self-created sustenance of a mind
> Debarr'd from Nature's living images,
> Compell'd to be a life unto itself,
> And unrelentingly possess'd by thirst
> Of greatness, love, and beauty.

VI. 305-316.

This is something beyond the circumfusing of " forms and substances with light divine." It draws from Plato's theory of ideas;
but does it not go beyond it?

We see, in this same sixth book of the *Prelude,* how Wordsworth extends his thinking to include the suggestion not only that the idea may be "so vivid that no visible observation could make it more so," but also, as we have observed, that bare reality may be inimical to the ideal. As he and his friend Robert Jones [5] pass through the changing "images and forms" on their progress toward Mt. Blanc, they develop an ideal of the mountain. It is the "monarch of mountains," heaven-baffling, stupendous. As they approach it they find it bulky, blunt, soulless. They are grieved; for the reality is nothing so glorious as the idea they had cherished.

> That day we first
> Beheld the summit of Mont Blanc, and griev'd
> To have a soulless image on the eye
> Which had usurp'd upon a living thought
> That never more could be.
>
> VI. 452-456.

This is desolating. It takes "five rivers broad and vast" and all the ethereal beauty of the Vale to compensate them for their intimate loss.

The mind, then, comes to a height at which it rejects the dominance of form. It only will be regnant, it the imperial, it ' the God-like, the creative.

> To every natural form, rock, fruit, or flower,
> Even the loose stones that cover the high-way
> I gave a moral life, I saw them feel.
>
> III. 124-126.

About himself the mature poet comes to make his own world. His eye no longer amid "all exterior forms" of stones, trees, leaves, or stars, can find a surface where its power may sleep. His mind above itself exalting itself, is no longer "prostrate, overborn, a mere pensioner On outward forms." It is indeed what he has called it, the "lord and master."

University of Michigan.

---

[5] In the long vacation of 1790, Robert Jones joined his friend Wordsworth in a walking tour through France and Switzerland.

WORDSWORTH: THE GROWTH OF A POET'S MIND

BENNETT WEAVER

I

ALWAYS approaching the mind of Wordsworth as poetic rather than philosophical, as a mind marked by imperial faculties rather than one subject to influences, we come to the most perplexing if not the profoundest problem in his work: the relationship existing between the mind and the materials with which the mind has to do. For the poet who wrote the early *Prelude* there were two worlds: the "visible universe" of the bodily eye; the visionary world of the "inward eye." In plain common sense we may well remember that these worlds exist naturally for man. They not only exist naturally, but the same mind which deals with the one works also in the other. There are, in short, not two minds in any man, but rather the one mind which functions now in perception and now in abstraction or creativity. The daffodils which to Dorothy and William "looked so gay, ever glancing, ever changing" became naturally for the poet

> The harvest of a quiet eye
> That broods and sleeps on his own heart.

Two worlds there are: the world "in the woods beyond Gowbarrow Park," and the world where the quiet eye reaps her harvest of beauty. The one Wordsworth perceived, the other he made. Without denying the act of perception we now seek especially to understand the potentiality by means of which the poet's mind creates.

Since the time when Hartley erected a neat and inclusive system upon the premises of certain of the older philosophers, we have been assured that the mind has no innate ideas and must depend upon the senses to inform it. We have also been assured that the mind may inform the senses, causing the eye to see what the mind wishes to see and the ear to hear what the mind wishes to hear. We recognize in this second process the beginnings of fancy and imagination.

But beyond both of these levels of speculation there is a region in which Wordsworth's regental power most significantly manifests itself, the region of the invisible world revealed only when the light of sense goes out. The first two levels of experience may be explored in great part with little more than the compass of psychology in one's hand, for they are the levels of sensationism. But the last level may not be so explored, belonging as it does properly to the transcendental This level is the level of the ecstatic and of the mystic, the level of Wordsworth's most characteristic, important, and difficult accomplishment.

Before we begin the study of the working of our poet's mind on these three levels we should clearly understand that there is nothing strange or arbitrary about assuming that these levels exist; neither is there any need for assuming that a poetic intelligence before it may know them must be instructed by a philosophical intelligence. I am not denying that Wordsworth's mind may have been so instructed, nor am I setting any limits to that instruction; I am merely saying that we need not assume it. I ask merely that we treat the poetry as poetry, and that when we have discovered a sufficient cause for its being what it is we do not then pile extraneous cause upon sufficient cause until we can consider only the extraneous.

When we turn to the first serious work of the poet we find just what we find in the work of that very normal, although exquisitely gifted young man, Keats — a heavy richness of material brought in by the senses. In "An Evening Walk" and in *Descriptive Sketches*, affected as they are by imitation of Pope, Gray, Thomson, Dyer, Winchelsea, and others, sensuous perception has not yet been transmuted into thought. Especially is this true of the sprightly young sense of sight. The poet walks to see and he relishes describing what he sees even as a young poet naturally would. He does not bring his book, and bend his head over the pages of Hartley, and reason: I am now in that age in which a poet is supposed to pay special attention to the report of the senses, therefore I shall describe. If his work bears evidence of his being in the age of excessive sensitiveness it is for reasons much more profound, reasons that lay living and red in the nerves and fibers of his body. Perhaps the first critic of his work, the unknown writer in the *Analytical Review* of March, 1793, assumed the profounder reasons. Very sanely he remarks in these poems "the eye of a diligent observer, and the hand of an able copyist of Nature." He finds no "thread of narrative to connect the several descriptions . . . the diversified pictures." Here is an athletic play of the senses, especially the tyrannic sense of sight. It is keen, minute, crafty, and as eager for itself as it is in the Alfoxden Dorothy. This man needed no sister to give him eyes, although later he may have had his natural propensities stimulated both by her example and by her sympathy.

This strong sporting of the senses continues in the Lyrical Ballads. As a sentient being Wordsworth was alive to the "mighty world of eye and ear." Yet we must remember that it was not in exemplification of some theory of the senses and of the outer world that Wordsworth wrote his share of the Ballads. If we may trust him it was not to give poetic expression to the sensism of Hartley that he wrote, but rather "to ascertain how far the language of conversation in the middle and lower classes of society is adapted to the purposes of poetic pleasure." True, he held that the passions of humble and rustic people "are incorporated with the beautiful and permanent forms of nature," and he assumed that the language which expressed those passions, therefore, drew from "the best objects from which the best part of language is originally derived." But is this not rather a mystic theory of language than one perspicuously sensationistic? Might we not remember here that composition is "a harmony of that language which is implanted by nature in man," although we should be remembering not Hartley, but Longinus? Surely Wordsworth in the original Advertisement to *Lyrical Ballads*, and Coleridge in Chapter XIV of the *Biographia Literaria*, write plainly about the aesthetic purpose and the occasion for the Ballads, and surely neither of them says a word about sensism. Just as surely each does say that "a faithful adherence to the truth of nature" was intended; "subjects were to be chosen from ordinary life"; and such tales as that of Goody Blake were "founded on well-authenticated fact which happened in Warwickshire" or elsewhere. To this generally defined aesthetic purpose Wordsworth addressed at least twelve of his contributions; and among these it is hard to find incontrovertible evidence that any other motive entered into their composition. That other elements did enter into such poems as "Lines Written in Early Spring" and "Expostulation and Reply" must be admitted; and it must be admitted, also, that those elements seem to derive

from Hartley.   Yet if we study poetry and evaluate poetry we should
not fail to discriminate between such quatrains as these:

> (*a*)   The eye it cannot chuse but see,
>   We cannot bid the ear be still;
>   Our bodies feel, where'er they be,
>   Against, or with our will.

> (*b*)   She had a rustic, woodland air,
>   And she was wildly clad;
>   Her eyes were fair, and very fair,
>   — Her beauty made me glad.

While the first quatrain affords the scholar an open opportunity to
point out the influence of Hartley upon Wordsworth, it affords a far
smaller opportunity to make clear that the influence resulted in
verse of genuine quality.   In fact, it were more just to observe that
in this rhymed statement of sensism we find already that fatally dull
element which slowly spreading almost silenced the *Excursion*.   It
would have been better for Wordsworth had he known that rhyming
stuff of the meddling intellect, or giving pentameter flow to religious
or moral speculation, is not to achieve in poetry.   That there are
times when he did know it is manifest.   My purpose for the moment
is to point out that the critic who fixes great significance to philosophic
matter embedded cold within a poet's lines is doomed to illusion and
error by the same token that the poet was who left the matter there.
The author must sense and know the difference between such a line
as "We cannot bid the ear be still" and "Her beauty made me glad";
and so must the scholar.   That Wordsworth could not maintain the
distinction was at times fatal to him; that the critic should not maintain it would be fatal.   In the first case the law of truth is violated,
and with it the law of beauty.   There is no health in the line.   In the
second case the human heart by which we live announces her universal joy.

Although we cannot examine carefully all the work which is
antecedent to the *Prelude*, or contemporary with the earlier books,
there are two poems at which we must look with care, the *Recluse*
and the "Lines Composed a Few Miles above Tintern Abbey."
Both of them contain something of the quality which distinguishes
the more inspired portions of the *Prelude*, a quality which we seek
and seek to emphasize.   Yet the grandeur which strikes through
the *Recluse* is fitful and transient.   The verses rush up to exhaus-

tion and cease. They are flushed with assumption, not poised in accomplishment. Among the reasons that may have caused Wordsworth to leave them incomplete was the fact that through them he was attempting simultaneously to enter two regions of song, the main region of the mind and the lesser region of the external world. Being poetically aware that the Soul is "an impulse to herself" and may know "Beauty" as "a living Presence of the earth," he nevertheless sweeps into what seems to be an acquired metaphysical confusion, trusting to reveal how "the external World is fitted to the Mind." When we are told that the "high argument" of the poem is to be "the creation" which the "individual Mind" and the "external World" blending their forces are to accomplish, we not only recognize that we are reading metaphysics and not poetry, but we also realize that we are no longer in the "main region" of Wordsworth's song. Between the eight hundred fourth and the eight hundred fifth verses of this fragment there is a great space, and in this space the poetic spirit has departed and the "discerning intellect" has come in. The result, to me, is a painful artistic confusion. Wordsworth suffers here, as he always must, from the indigestible aliment he has filched from Locke and Hartley. He no longer feeds his soul with the communion bread taken from the altars of the Presence and he becomes a sick artist. Yet the significance of the *Recluse* lies unmistakably not in the palsied passages which argue out the spousal hymn of the mind and not-mind, but in the vital passages which declare Wordsworth's blood brotherhood with the man who had neither opportunity nor need to read Locke and Hartley, John Milton. When we look for "the lord and master" of Wordsworth's poetry we do not find him paging Hartley beneath the red light of sense, but enthroned rather with other great poets under the radiance of "dread infinitude." And we should remember what Dante knew:

> It may not be
> That one, who looks upon that light, can turn
> To other object, willingly, his view.

When we come to the famous "Lines" composed on July 13, 1798, we are aware of a lower and a higher level of work, the one which may be approached by the steppingstones of influences, the other which can be entered upon only when we remember that this great man really had a mind of his own with certain distinct and absolute powers. Two sweeping passages in the poem declare these powers.

Each rushes up into poetry of the higher kind, each breaks at the peak into more than can be explained by the determinable elements which seem to make it up. The first of these lies between lines twenty-two and forty-nine, the second lies between lines fifty and one hundred seven. Each of them exploits sensism; each of them goes beyond it. It is the "going beyond" which we must observe.

Let us turn to the poem:

> that serene and blessed mood,
> In which the affections gently lead us on, —
> Until, the breath of this corporeal frame
> And even the motion of our human blood
> Almost suspended, we are laid asleep
> In body, and become a living soul:
> While with an eye made quiet by the power
> Of harmony, and the deep power of joy,
> We see into the life of things.   (41–49)

How can we read this as poetry and not know that the essential experience referred to here is vital and not derivative; and that, since it is ecstatic, it belongs to the poet himself? No ecstatic experience is derivative, nor can it be properly spoken of as being so; for it is instant, personal, "closer than hands and feet." This it is to be "laid asleep In body, and become a living soul"; and this it must be before the poet shall "see into the life of things." In the intellectual rationalism that derives from Aristotle there is nothing of quality sufficiently similar to these lines to give them adequate explanation. Let us read on.

> And I have felt
> A presence that disturbs me with the joy
> Of elevated thoughts; a sense sublime
> Of something far more deeply interfused,
> Whose dwelling is the light of setting suns,
> And the round ocean and the living air,
> And the blue sky, and in the mind of man:
> A motion and a spirit, that impels
> All thinking things, all objects of all thought,
> And rolls through all things. Therefore am I still
> A lover of the meadows and the woods,
> And mountains; and of all that we behold
> From this green earth; of all the mighty world
> Of eye, and ear, — both what they half create,
> And what perceive.   (93–107)

If one were to give plain expression to the poetic concept adumbrated in these lines, the paraphrase might read like this: Because one common spirit dwells in the mind and in the fair works of nature, the mind loves — for the sake of this spirit — all objects of the not-mind. Since the same spirit which is in the mind is in the meadow and the woods, the mind loves them, senses a pleasant, instant, and intimate communion of its life with their life. Deep calleth unto deep; and it is as if the common spirit grew happily aware of itself, conscious of itself in the one and in the other. There is no more near nor far. It can make no difference, then — and here we must be alert and aware of the fact that perchance we attempt to make clear what Wordsworth yearned to say but could not quite since a philosophical concept hung like an interdict upon his spirit — it can make no difference whether the mind creates the mighty world out of itself, or through perception receives the mighty world into itself; for in either case the common presence is exercising itself in the joy of self-contemplation. And here we note a profound aesthetic implication: the mind is not passive in relation to the senses, but passive only to the all-pervading Presence. Being passive to the all-pervading Presence, by subtle qualities of paradox in that spirit, it is made to participate in the creative and imperial power of the Presence. To this height of suggestion had Wordsworth's poetic inspiration lifted him.

But he was not able entirely to keep his poise near the thundering Jehovah and among the "choir Of shouting Angels." In the one hundred third verse there is a dull slackening, a change from the rapt contemplation of the unific omnipresence to a reasoned statement. "Therefore am I still" is not instinct with the poetic spirit. The intellect begins to meddle. Through the exhaustion of the contemplative and creative faculties it insinuates itself — with what result? The imaginative powers shrink further inward and, to a mind no longer able to furnish itself with materials for its own work, mere memory presents the strange and untransmutable lines from Edward Young's *Night Thoughts* (VI, 425):

> And half create the wondrous world they see;
> Our senses, as our reason, are divine.

So Wordsworth forsakes himself, confessing his weakness and confusion in the words,

> of all the mighty world
> Of eye, and ear — both what they half create,
> And what perceive.

For the rest of the poem he comes down dizzily into sensism. A pathetic falseness steals into his work, in nothing more poignant than in his assuring Dorothy that "Nature never did betray The Heart that Loved her," and that her mind should "be a mansion for all lovely forms." I cannot read this part of the poem without a feeling of pain other than that one should receive from true art. For the feeling is that the poet has betrayed himself and has failed in his true gift, the gift of penetration "into the life of things." I feel that he has justly, although unconsciously, laid himself open to the derision of the years. A poet in his true place should grasp the future in the instant. And in what does his failure announce itself? In the language of sensism:

> Well pleased to recognize
> In nature and the language of the sense
> The anchor of my purest thoughts, the nurse,
> The guide, the guardian of my heart, and soul
> Of all my moral being.   (107-111)

In relation to the poet's high experience these lines are spurious and their assurance is mockery. We do him wrong to seek in his re-phrasing of another man's thought his own best meaning. We do ourselves wrong when we find his significance outside those passages in which he maintains his earnest integrity.

II

As we pass into a study of the *Prelude* we recall Harper's statement suggesting that the first two books "were probably finished before the close of 1800. The poem was then laid aside until the spring of 1804." We expect, then, to find a generous similarity between the first two books and the poems we have just discussed; but, although we may expect a strong continuance of sensism in these books we may also anticipate in the later divisions of the poem changes toward a higher quality of thought. These changes are the more probable since in the Preface of 1802 Wordsworth seems fully to have exploited if not to have exhausted his ability to accept a philosophical doctrine fundamentally foreign to his poetic genius. That the poet was in youth almost fiercely alive to the senses, sinking up and down in their crested turbulence, is true; and that he thought to give this very aliveness explicability by confining it in the frames and molds of another's terminology seems true; but it is also certain that these frames and molds could not hold his full mind and that, therefore, the richest significance of his work is not in them.

We have been made aware of this last truth as we have come through the first book. The disciplines of beauty and of fear, however much they may remind us of Locke's disciplines of "love and fear, as the great principles," principles which were so sweetly applied to young Basil Montagu at Racedown, ever conclude in characteristic abstractions. An "undetermin'd sense Of unknown modes of being" ending at last in "blank desertion" of the senses and fearfully tense brooding while "huge and mighty Forms" move through his mind with oppressive slowness — these are the distinctive experiences of the poet put before us with repetitious insistence. What he has clearly emphasized is that in his boyhood the most significant experiences of his mind, those, in fact, which made him poet, were experiences which, however initiated through the senses, came to transcend them utterly. These high moments in his youth were the true harbingers of the "spots of time" which in his later years left him assured that he was one of the "hierophants of the unapprehended beauty of the universe."

Then, too, as we read in the second book that passage which is most akin to the second portion of the "Lines" which we have remarked, we find in it not only the familiar confusion which the poet recognizes and tries to eliminate in later recensions, but we find also an awareness of the creative power of the mind and of the transcendent quality of abstraction.

> Bless'd the infant Babe,
> (For with my best conjectures I would trace
> The progress of our Being) blest the Babe,
> Nurs'd in his Mother's arms, the Babe who sleeps
> Upon his Mother's breast, who, when his soul
> Claims manifest kindred with an earthly soul,
> Doth gather passion from his Mother's eye!
> Such feelings pass into his torpid life
> Like an awakening breeze, and hence his mind
> Even in the first trial of its powers
> Is prompt and watchful, eager to combine
> In one appearance, all the elements
> And parts of the same object, else detach'd
> And loth to coalesce. Thus, day by day,
> Subjected to the discipline of love,

> His organs and recipient faculties
> Are quicken'd, are more vigorous, his mind spreads . . .
> From nature largely he receives; nor so
> Is satisfied, but largely gives again.   (II, 237–268) [1]

One is indeed left unsure of the meaning of these verses. The poet has just admitted, in deference to honesty and good sense, that no one "knows the individual hour in which His habits were first sown," and having admitted this, he seems to continue under the doom of philosophical sentimentality. His "best conjectures" cannot appease his plain intelligence; and after an ineffectual struggle with "organs and recipient faculties" he succeeds more in leaving his reader "bewilder'd and depress'd" than in writing good poetry. The "torpid life" of the little associationist spreads throughout the verses themselves. For an instant Wordsworth rises toward the idea familiar to us in the *Recluse* and the "Lines," the idea that the mind is

> creator and receiver both,
> Working but in alliance with the works
> Which it beholds.   (II, 273–275)

Then he gathers himself for the poetic recapitulation of what he has failed to make poetic, and succeeds only in pronouncing that "this infant sensibility" is the "Great birthright of our Being." We are amazed to be told immediately that the author has descried "a path More difficult" before him up which he is bent to go. Yet his instinct is right; for he means to rise above associationism. His honesty triumphs:

> Yet is a path
> More difficult before me, and I fear
> That in its broken windings we shall need
> The chamois' sinews, and the eagle's wing;
> For now a trouble came into my mind
> From unknown causes. I was left alone,
> Seeking the visible world, nor knowing why.
>   (II, 287–293)

This trouble, like that in the pool of Bethesda, has the power to cure. Again Wordsworth becomes the poet, "whole as the casing air."

As in the "Lines" we find him "laid asleep In body, and become a living soul," so in the second book, we find him erecting himself above the fatally neat molds of sensism into which he has tried to run his mind.

[1] Quotations are from the 1805 *Prelude*, edited by de Selincourt.

> Before the vernal thrush
> Was audible, among the hills I sate
> Alone, upon some jutting eminence
> At the first hour of morning, when the Vale
> Lay quiet in an utter solitude.
> How shall I trace the history, where seek
> The origin of what I then have felt?
> Oft in these moments such a holy calm
> Did overspread my soul, that I forgot
> That I had bodily eyes, and what I saw
> Appear'd like something in myself, a dream,
> A prospect in my mind.   (II, 360–371)

These lines, although they did not satisfy their author, are authentic, pristine stuff. In just such places and at just such times Wordsworth sat, no book in hand; with just such honesty he would question any attempt to name the origins of poetic feeling, although his whole poem might falsely be said to be given to that very task; and into just such abstraction he would naturally rise. For him, "O'er all that moves, O'er all, that, to the human eye Invisible, yet liveth, O'er all that leaps, and runs, and shouts, and sings" rises a song of transport, audible,

> Most audible then when the fleshly ear,
> O'ercome by grosser prelude of that strain,
> Forgot its functions, and slept undisturb'd.
>   (II, 432–434)

Wordsworth not only experiences the inadequacy of the senses, but also, having experienced that inadequacy, turns with justified suspicion against them. For the very reason that he is so sharply alive to them, he feels the danger of their tyranny. He knows that if he pauses with them, or stops in the satisfaction of what they may do, he is no poet but a self-sufficing thing to whom a primrose will be a primrose and nothing more. Pressing instantly and forever upon him is the artistic necessity for escaping the thraldom of Acrasia. Having observed that the body and the mind make up "A twofold Frame," and that man has "two natures" that must be kept "in wholesome separation," the poet is keenly aware that the senses grown despotic war with the heart and subjugate the mind. Nature herself, knowing this, "summons all the senses each To counteract the other and themselves," only thus being able to keep them subservient; and subservient they must be kept if the "inner faculties" so vital to the poet are not to be "laid asleep." The mind that is "truly from the Deity" may be "quicken'd, rouz'd, and made thereby more apt to hold communion with the invisible world"; but the poet must beware

> The tendency, too potent in itself,
> Of habit to enslave the mind, I mean
> Oppress it by the laws of vulgar sense,
> And substitute a universe of death,
> The falsest of all worlds, in place of that
> Which is divine and true.
> (XIII, 138–143)

It is right to say that Wordsworth has learned from Hartley; but it is not right to leave unsaid that the most vital thing he learned from him is the inadequacy of his system. The philosopher falls short of the poet and would, if unrepudiated and untranscended, be as inimical to him as the coarse and vulgar sense is to the mind and soul. The Wordsworth of 1804 writes a forceful paradox against the whole matter.

> Great God!
> That aught *external* to the living mind
> Should have such mighty sway!
> (VIII, 699–700)

And these words are assurance enough that the sway was sufficiently mitigated.

For two reasons, probably, the senses play a lesser and a more regulated part in those books of the *Prelude* written after the February of 1804 than they do in those written before that time. Obviously, in treating the more mature years of his life, when the animal appetites were quieted by thought and when his body no longer drank in the very stillness about it, he would give less place and emphasis to the study of the senses. Obviously, also, since he writes these books in the period of his maturity, he is more disposed to call attention to the deceptive and the inimical aspects of the senses. Supplementing both these reasons is the fact that along with the deeper understanding of his mind the poet has gained a greater sureness and self-respect as an artist. Even in the presence of the Alps, "magnificent region," he insists that he is

> Not prostrate, overborn, as if the mind
> Itself were nothing, a mean pensioner
> On outward forms.   (VI, 666–668)

And then with wholesome dignity and clear assertion he adds:

> On the front
> Of this whole Song is written that my heart
> Must in such temple needs have offer'd up
> A different worship.   (VI, 669–672)

How had Wordsworth come to the necessity of offering up a different worship? By a long pilgrimage from the East where gleams of light fell often upon him, "Gleams like the flashing of a shield." While he walked the visible world, flashes came to him from the invisible. The mighty world of eye and ear began to be superseded by the mightier world of the mind. About him now spread a light that never was on land or sea. He remembered the hour of his dedication when he was staid utterly beneath the memorable pomp and glory of the morning. His soul was rapt away into the infinite and when it returned to him it was invested with an auxiliar light. He had the poet's power to add beauty unto beauty. Upon the top of Snowdon a light falls with a flash, and the poet gazes deep into the life of things, and out upon "The Soul, the Mighty Mind, the Power Invisible." So it is that he was schooled as an artist and as a poet enabled to say in the very presence of the Alps:

> To my Soul I say
> I recognize thy glory; in such strength
> Of usurpation, in such visitings
> Of awful promise, when the light of sense
> Goes out in flashes that have shewn to us
> The invisible world, doth Greatness make abode,
> There harbours whether we be young or old.
> Our destiny, our nature, and our home
> Is with infinitude, and only there. (VI, 531–539)

This was spoken with integrity, and like a true poet. We have passed the point beyond the instant; we have passed from the senses that deal with the visible world to the mind that lives in the invisible. It is with the strong workings of this mind that we must associate the great Wordsworth, the poet who sank deep, rose high "to where the heaven of heavens is but a veil."

However, even in the high experiences of the "spots of time" Wordsworth does not utterly deny sense, he merely holds it in its proper position. To know that there is an invisible world is not perforce to deny the visible. So all aesthetic knowledge would heap

the world with ignorance and come to baffle itself.   Yet, since April 4,
1802, Wordsworth has been familiar with these verses of his friend:

> O William! we receive but what we give,
> And in our life alone does Nature live. . . .
>   Ah! from the soul itself must issue forth
> A light, a glory, a fair luminous cloud
>   Enveloping the Earth.

Perhaps, as I suggested, it was in 1802 that he began to move forward through the vortex of sensism toward the light of the mind.
At any rate, in the ninth book we find what I have called the significant poet, working at last in his own genius.

> This efficacious spirit chiefly lurks
> Among those passages of life in which
> We have had deepest feeling that the mind
> Is lord and master, and that outward sense
> Is but the obedient servant of her will.
> (XI, 269–273)

The poet has now shaken off the confusion which was upon him when
he wrote the *Recluse*.   He is free for vision and for contemplation.
Perhaps he is not entirely free since he is not always free; and yet,
although his mind may not be pervaded by a steady and lasting
clarity, it has become lord and master of the senses.

UNIVERSITY OF MICHIGAN

WORDSWORTH: THE AESTHETIC INTIMATION

By BENNETT WEAVER

The aesthetic intimation of spiritual truth came early to the mind of Wordsworth. "Fair seed time had my soul," he wrote, "and I grew up Foster'd alike by beauty and by fear." As a mature artist he bears tribute to the "beauteous" Derwent, "the fairest of all Rivers," which blended its murmurs with his nurse's song. With this "dearly lov'd Playmate" he, as "a five year's Child," sported the long summer's day. But beauty might not come alone to his mind; for within the aesthetic experience fear also has her place. The "loud dry wind" must speak across the crag, and "grim shapes" must tower between him and the stars. Beauty must be aided by her sister, Sublimity. Not to separate beauty and sublimity is Wordsworth's deepest wisdom.

Having been thus nourished in his earlier years, Wordsworth shows no astonishment when he comes upon the maturing abilities of his mind. He has not been long at Cambridge before on "moonlight nights" he gazes out of his window at the statue "Of Newton, with his Prism and silent Face." He is lost stealthily in a high companionship. Does not his mind, also, voyage through "strange seas of thought alone"? Surely there is a strangeness in his mind, a sense of high destiny.

I was a chosen Son.
For hither I had come with holy powers
And faculties, whether to work or feel: . . .
I was a Freeman; in the purest sense
Was free, and to majestic ends was strong. . . .
I look'd for universal things; perused
The common countenance of earth and heaven;
And, turning the mind in upon itself,
Pored, watch'd, expected, listen'd; spread my thoughts
And spread them with a wider creeping; felt
Incumbencies more awful, visitings
Of the Upholder of the tranquil Soul,
Which Underneath all passions lives secure
A steadfast life. But peace! it is enough
To notice that I was ascending now
To such community with highest truth. . . .
I had a world about me; 'twas my own,
I made it; for it only liv'd to me,
And to the God who look'd into my mind.

Such sympathies would sometimes shew themselves
By outward gestures and by visible looks.
Some call'd it madness: such, indeed, it was. . . .
If prophecy be madness. . . .
Of Genius, Power,
Creation and Divinity itself
I have been speaking. (*The Prelude* [1805], III, 79-173.)

It is not our purpose to exhaust the significance of these lines. For this moment we fix our attention upon the intense self-consciousness which prepares the intelligence for "community with highest truth." I have no doubt that we have in these verses as clear a record of the maturing of the aesthetic consciousness to the state in which it may receive the fruitful intimations of the immortal as we shall find in our literature. By the shock of leaving his mountain home and coming to an academic place, some power is roused in the poet. Melancholy rises among his thoughts and a strangeness comes suddenly among them. He is one chosen. His faculties and powers are holy. The infinite pouring itself into the finite has filled him with a divine madness.

> O Heavens! how awful is the might of Souls,
> And what they do within themselves,

he cries. Then, feeling the breath of the incommunicable upon him, he suddenly concludes: "Enough: for now We must descend."

As rich in confession as this passage is and as full of marvel as it is, there is in it no reference to that instantaneous and consummating experience which is the next phase in the growth of poetic genius. Not wishing to distingush in quality between aesthetic rapture and religious ecstasy, I wish only to indicate an experience in which magnificence embosoms the poetic being with such warmth that an eternal positiveness is engendered within it. Out of the fertile moment of beauty and sublimity, comes an assurance of the infinite. First the magnificence, the pomp, and the glory, and then the stillness and the vow.

> Magnificent
> The morning was, in memorable pomp,
> More glorious than I ever had beheld.
> The Sea was laughing at a distance; all
> The solid Mountains were as bright as clouds,
> Grain-tinctured, drench'd in empyrean light; . . .
> —Ah! need I say, dear Friend, that to the brim
> My heart was full; I made no vows, but vows
> Were then made for me; bond unknown to me
> Was given, that I should be, else sinning greatly,
> A dedicated Spirit. (IV, 330-344.)

The marked characteristic of these lines is that Wordsworth is not making the vows but that the vows are made for him. The poet is not making his claim upon the infinite, but the infinite is making its claim upon the poet. Further, the earlier verses of this passage which prepare us for the dedication, are ''drench'd in empyrean light.'' Anyone thinking for a moment will recognize the peculiar significance which Wordsworth gives to light, associating it with the very spirit of creativity. The fire in the bush had scarcely more authority with Moses than ''the light that never was, on sea or land'' had with Wordsworth. To him the poet is a shining being; and at the hour of his own consecration the very mountains are drenched in light. And finally, whereas Shelley, struck by the sudden Shadow, shrieks and clasps his hands in ecstasy, Wordsworth experiences a strong calm which remains with him so long as he is worthy of himself.

> On I walk'd
> In blessedness, which even yet remains.

In its treatment of magnificence, in its knowledge of aesthetic passivity, in its record of the calm that follows dedication this passage is as authentic as any in all of Wordsworth.

However, before Wordsworth can follow on the way which leads from the holiness of beauty to the beauty of holiness, he has a battle to fight with sense. Already having the propensity of the poet to delight in ''the mighty world Of eye, and ear,'' he finds ready-made the systematic explanations of the relation of that world to his mind as they were developed by Hartley and Alison. It is inevitable that these systems make a deep impression on him; and yet, even as we say this, we must be aware of two things. The first of these is that the more closely one man quotes another the more he may be indicating a native sympathy rather than admitting an influence. The second of these is that the system of sensism is more honored by the young man than by the matured poet. Quite simply, the play of the senses is strong in the young Wordsworth, just as it was in the ''sensuous'' Milton and is in Keats. Not so simply, but understandably, when that play of youth becomes the work of maturity, the senses are remanded to their due place and the system falls off like a dry shell. If to make too simple is the Scylla of criticism, to make strange, complex, and difficult is the Charybdis. The palpable fact in the case of Wordsworth is that despite his long struggle with sensism his deeper and truer genius was all the while enlisted against such an inadequate philosophy.

There comes a time, shortly after his dedication, when Wordsworth begins to experience that exquisite listlessness of the senses which leaves the body ''drinking in the stillness'' of solitude. The quiescent consciousness of ''an exhausted mind'' approaches a condition of trance in which there rise far streaming pageantries. Sensibility grows weaker and weaker in its restraint of the imaginative power. Chant as he will the spousal verse of ''the individual Mind'' and ''the external World,'' and talk as he will of the ''organs and recipient faculties'' of ''the infant Babe,'' and celebrate as he will ''infant sensibility'' as the ''Great birthright of our Being,'' the poet knows that ''the Mind of Man'' is the haunt and the main region of his song—

> Beauty— a living Presence of the earth,
> Surpassing the most fair ideal Forms
> Which craft of delicate Spirits hath composed
> From earth's materials. (*The Recluse*, 795-798.)

He knows well enough that although the senses may inform the mind, the mind may inform the senses or transcend them altogether.

In the second book of the *Prelude*, shortly after he has paid his devoirs to ''infant sensibility,'' Wordsworth writes a passage which reminds us of Saint Teresa's ''orison of union,'' that state in which ''the soul is fully awake as regards God, but wholly asleep as regards things of this world and in respect of herself.'' A ''trouble'' comes into the mind of the poet. It arises ''From unknown causes.''

> I was left alone,
> Seeking the visible world, nor knowing why.
> The props of my affections were remov'd,
> And yet the building stood, as if sustain'd
> By its own spirit! (II, 292-296.)

He is left alone in the invisible world; the support of the senses is taken away from his affections. By all the laws of sensism and of associationism the affections should fall, and yet they stand! Validities seem to shift; he questions and is troubled. But the answer comes to him after he has grown for two more years, after he has ''crossed the Alps.'' Give Wordsworth but time and he will explain himself to himself. Observe how similar this following passage is to that which we have just quoted, and yet how different.

> I was lost as in a cloud,
> Halted, without a struggle to break through.

> And now recovering, to my Soul I say
> I recognize thy glory; . . .
> when the light of sense
> Goes out in flashes that have shewn to us
> The invisible world.   (VI, 529-536.)

Having remarked the significant "dissimilitude in similitude" in these verses of Book II and of Book VI, we should notice that the first passage was written in 1802, descriptive of an experience in early childhood; that the second passage was written in 1804, descriptive of an experience at the age of twenty. We may assume that the difference in the lines is attributable to either or to both of these facts. We may perhaps help ourselves in understanding the poet's progress to the place where "the light of sense Goes out" by returning to *Tintern Abbey* and then observing two other passages in the second book of the *Prelude*.

Remembering that in 1802 it was the props of his *affections* which had been removed and that in 1804 he came to recognize the glory of his *soul*, let us read the familiar lines written in 1798:—

> That serene and blessed mood,
> In which the affections gently lead us on,–
> Until, the breath of our corporeal frame
> And even the motion of our human blood
> Almost suspended, we are laid asleep
> In body, and become a living soul:
> While with an eye made quiet by the power
> Of harmony, and the deep power of joy,
> We see into the life of things.   (41-49.)

If these words had been written in 1804, would scholars find in them a precipitation of sensism or a suggestion of mysticism? Had William James, not bothering his judgment with chronology, analyzed the verses, what might he have concluded? "We are wholly asleep as regards the things of this world," says Teresa; "We are laid asleep in body," says Wordsworth. "The soul is fully awake," says Teresa; "We become a living soul," says Wordsworth. Here are two things equally difficult: To prove that Teresa was a follower of Hartley and to prove that Wordsworth was a follower of Teresa! Let us leave the matter, then, and go on to the first of the two other passages from the second book of the *Prelude*.

In this passage we find the poet "alone" just as he was described as being in verse 292 of Book II and in verse 529 of Book VI. We find, also, that he is seeking to trace the origin of what he felt, just as he was in *Tintern*. We find, further, the same however-induced state of suspension and calm; and it is early morning, just as it was at the time of the poet's "call."

> Before the vernal thrush
> Was audible, among the hills I sate
> Alone, upon some jutting eminence
> At the first hour of morning, when the Vale
> Lay quiet in an utter solitude.
> How shall I trace the history, where seek
> The origin of what I then have felt?
> Oft (sic!) in these moments such a holy calm
> Did overspread my soul, that I forgot
> That I had bodily eyes, and what I saw
> Appear'd like something in myself, a dream,
> A prospect in my mind.   (II, 360-371.)

Again, as in *Tintern* his eye was "made quiet by the power Of harmony, and the deep power of joy," so now he sees one harmonious life in all things and feels that it is joy. Furthermore he expressly indicates the suspension of the senses.

> Wonder not
> If such my transports were; for in all things now
> I saw one life, and felt that it was joy.
> One song they sang, and it was audible,
> Most audible then when the fleshly ear,
> O'ercome by grosser prelude of that strain,
> Forgot its functions, and slept undisturbed.   (II, 428-434.)

This is close to hearing "the inner sound which kills the outer— THE VOICE OF THE SILENCE."

The meaning of these passages in themselves is indubitable, and their significance is not hidden. They bring us on fairly to the place where the light of sense goes out in flashes that reveal the invisible world. If it be the business of the poet to see into the life of things, then he must look with "the inner eye"; if it be his business to hear the song of joy at the heart of life, then he must listen with something other than "the fleshly ear." And hence it comes that the physical senses are inadequate to the poet, and being inadequate are therefore inimical. They make the mind

> As if the mind
> Itself were nothing, a mean pensioner
> On outward forms.   (VI, 666-668.)

Nature herself puts forth a power over them in order that the poet, "By sensible impressions not enthrall'd (XIII, 103)," may exercise "the glorious faculty" of creativity, the faculty "Which higher minds bear with them as their own (XIII, 90)." Especially does Nature discipline "The most despotic of our senses," the eye, which aspires to gain mastery of the heart and to hold the mind "In absolute dominion." In order that man may grow, escaping the "thraldom of that sense" (XI, 198), Nature,

> To thwart
> This tyranny, summons all the senses each
> To counteract the other and themselves. (XI, 179-181.)

With an intensity and a brusqueness that indicate finality Wordsworth condemns every combination of the senses

> That might aid
> The tendency, too potent in itself,
> Of habit to enslave the mind, I mean
> Oppress it by the laws of vulgar sense,
> And substitute a universe of death,
> The falsest of all worlds, in place of that
> Which is divine and true. (XIII, 137-143.)

To speak of the man who sees the world of sense as "the falsest of all worlds, a universe of death," as one who accepts the system of Hartley, even to the willful blunting of his poetic powers, is to speak fantastically. If there is a stiffer repudiation of sensism written in our English literature before 1850 I do not know it. Regardless of all that Wordsworth may have drawn from Hartley, we do not adequately remark upon what he learned from the associationistic philosopher until we say that the chief thing which he learned was to repudiate him.

We are now in a better position to see how, in the case of Wordsworth, the aesthetic fulfilled itself in the spiritual. The exquisite sensitiveness of his early years left him more aware of the *je ne sais quoi* beyond the senses than finally accommodated within the dead order of a philosophical system. The need and the urge which lead Wordsworth into sensism lead him through it and out of it. In the course of nature many a quick and gifted mind, lost for a period among indeterminate certainties and whirling comprehensions, affects the rational and steadies itself with perception. It is a state of apparent atheism subject to the startling purges of beauty; and in the normal process of growth some hour will come when beauty will make the mind hale and ready for infinitude. What seems to be and is indeed the instant of readiness has been prepared by a long labor; and the rapture which seems to deny anticipation lies clear among the laws of expectancy.

We return now for one more reading of the lines in the third book which memorialize the poet's assurance of his "holy powers." Having found in them a record of the maturing of the aesthetic consciousness to the state in which it might receive the intimations of the immortal, we have now to treat briefly the consequent apprehension of "Divinity itself." As the young poet spread out his thoughts for fearful scrutiny, he felt among them

> Incumbencies more awful, visitings
> Of the Upholder of the tranquil Soul.

Underneath all his passions he found this Upholder living "A steadfast life." He could not more openly claim that God was in his mind. And he instances the fundamental similarity between his mind and that of the invasive Presence. Is God a creative spirit? The poet is also a creator.

> I had a world about me; 'twas my own,
> I made it; for it only liv'd to me,
> And to the God who look'd into my mind.

Here speaks the poet who six years earlier knew that he must ascend aloft and

> Breathe in worlds
> To which the heaven of heavens is but a veil.
> All strength—all terror, single or in bands,
> That ever was put forth in personal form—
> Jehovah—with his thunder, and the choir
> Of shouting Angels, and the empyreal thrones—
> I pass them unalarmed.   (*The Recluse*, 29-35.)

These lines may offend Blake and deserve from Keats the shrewd appelative "egotistical Sublime"; but as poetry they are perspicuous. And in 1804, Wordsworth with measured emphasis, reiterates his claim upon sublimity.

> Of Genius, Power,
> Creation and Divinity itself
> I have been speaking.

If we may think of the spiritual as that which has to do with Divinity, we see Wordsworth here in the act of passing out of the aesthetic into the spiritual. Had Haydon caught the vision of these lines, he would on his great canvas have set beneath the face of Keats the face of another young man with eyes lifted and glittering with light.

Among the *Ecclesiastical Sonnets* I find one bearing this apposite title: *The Point at Issue*. It poses the question that pours the aesthetic into the spiritual, and gives the answer to the act.

> For what contend the wise?—for nothing less
> Than that the Soul, freed from the bonds of Sense,

> And to her God restored by evidence
> Of things not seen, drawn forth from their recess,
> Root there, and not in forms, her holiness.   (1-5.)

These lines, as poetry, are not thrilling; but they are thrilling in idea, and tend greatly to establish the thesis of our study. At once they demolish the right to speak of Wordsworth as one who hardened into a senile formalism. They repeat the distinction between sense and spirit, a need more than adumbrated in the *Prelude* and one given rational explanation in the *Excursion*. But more than all else they restore the soul ''to her God'' by an act of that faith which is best defined as ''Imagination in her most exalted mood.'' The active powers of man are released, and

> They sweep distemper from the busy day,
> And make the chalice of the big round year
> Run o'er with gladness; whence the Being moves
> In beauty through the world.   (*Excursion*, IX, 131-136.)

University of Michigan

WORDSWORTH'S *PRELUDE*: THE SHAPING SPIRIT

By Bennett Weaver

In our study of the *Prelude* we have remembered that we are dealing with a " meditative History, the history of a Poet's mind," and that in an essential way the history of a mind is different from the biographical record of a life. We are now ready to follow the " main essential Power " of that mind " up her way sublime." At the beginning, however, we can do nothing better than to set firmly beneath our feet a statement which Wordsworth makes regarding this Power. After speaking of divine love which proceeds from " the brooding Soul," the poet continues:

> This love more intellectual cannot be
> Without Imagination, which, in truth,
> Is but another name for absolute strength
> And clearest insight, amplitude of mind,
> And reason in her most exalted mood.
> This faculty hath been the moving soul
> Of our long labor: we have traced the stream
> From darkness, and the very place of birth
> In its blind cavern, whence is faintly heard
> The sound of waters; follow'd it to light
> And open day, accompanied its course
> Among the ways of Nature, afterwards
> Lost sight of it bewilder'd and engulph'd,
> Then given it greeting, as it rose once more
> With strength, reflecting in its solemn breast
> The works of man and face of human life,
> And lastly, from its progress have we drawn
> The feeling of life endless, the great thought
> By which we live, Infinity and God.   XIII. 166-184.

Although we are to explore these lines, we can assure ourselves at the outset that Wordsworth conceives of imagination as " the moving soul " of the *Prelude*. It is a power absolute and exalted; it is the shaping spirit by which all is wrought. Lost in its beginning within the infinite, its progress is a vast returning " Among the ways of Nature " and " The works of man " until it rests once more within its source. It is not the mind, but a power within the mind which can see into the life of things and may participate in " the eternal act of creation."

In our study of this power we must follow the poet; and we must not claim more skill than he, or greater sapience. When he states that in no mystic sense but in plain reason no one can point out the source of the poetic spirit, we must defer to his honesty. When he, upon the stretch to make his matter clear, cries: " Hard task! It lies far hidden from the reach of words!" we must not offer an easy explanation. Where he stops without an effort to break through, we must also pause. If at last laboring under the infinitude of his inspiration he gives to some symbol a meaning which plain words cannot carry, then as we are able we must let that symbol illuminate our minds. Knowing that we shall partly fail in the exposition of the deepest truth, we must nevertheless do what we can.

In reading the second book of the *Prelude,* which was probably written two years after the " Lines Composed Above Tintern Abbey " and in the same year with the *Recluse,* we come upon a passage dealing with " the first Poetic spirit of our human life." We find this spirit using the " organs and recipient faculties " of the " infant Babe; " and we are told that he,

> Even as an agent of the one great mind,
> Creates, creator and receiver both,
> Working, but in alliance with the work
> Which [he] beholds. II. 272-275.

These lines have in them an incompleteness similar to that which we may note in Tintern and the *Recluse,*[1] an incompleteness that results in a falsity about which we must be clear before we can understand the imagination. For the poetic spirit cannot in the last assay serve both sense and imagination: it must *in the last assay* either hate the one or love the other. The confusion over this issue in Wordsworth's own thought was stubborn and deep. His genius was to serve the imagination; but he sometimes denied his own intelligence in assuming the philosophy of sensism. If, as Hartley maintains, the mind can create only with and by means of what it receives through the senses, then creativity is absolutely dependent upon the senses. Ultimately there can be no innate power; since power to be must express itself. Imagination, then,

---

[1] I refer to lines 105-107 of Tintern with which compare Young's *Night Thoughts,* VI. 425, 426, and to lines 805-824 of the *Recluse.*

which can work only with materials deposited by the senses, cannot be innate or divine. If, seriously, the "agent of the one great mind" can do nothing except it be in alliance with external objects, then the agent differs essentially from the mind which is serves. For it is *the* characteristic of the "one great mind" to create, to require only void into which it may cast the sudden shapes of its own being. By putting objects before mind and substance before the Creator the poet has denied his own nature and walked out backward into the dark place of philosophical confusion.

But Wordsworth does not remain in confusion. When a strong man wrestles with a problem he gives of his force to the problem until it seems greater than it is. Just so the speculations on sensism seem to gain a fullness of import in this mind, although the special gift of the mind is visionary power. Let us immediately begin our journey toward "the light of open day" by recalling what Wordsworth wrote to Wrangham in the January of 1816: "Throughout [*The White Doe*], objects derive their influence, not from properties inherent in them, not from what they ARE actually in themselves, but from such as are bestowed upon them by the minds of those who are conversant with or affected by those objects. Thus THE POETRY, if there be any in the work, PROCEEDS, as it ought to do, FROM THE SOUL OF MAN, COMMUNICATING ITS CREATIVE ENERGIES to the images of the external world."

Surely this private remark is free of obfuscation. By using the device of ITALICS one can make it obvious that Wordsworth was not most significantly the poet of "wise passiveness," but one of a much wiser activeness. The source of poetry—and there can be no questioning Wordsworth's meaning—is not the objective world, neither is it the sense by means of which the objective world invades the mind; the source of poetry is in the soul, the imperial, the creative.

This truth was at earlier times clear to Wordsworth even in the less impassioned moments of the *Prelude*. In the seventh book he is speaking of the spectacles which in London lay about him.

> Though rear'd upon the base of outward things,
> These, chiefly, are such structures as the mind
> Builds for itself. Scenes different there are,
> Full-form'd, which take, with small internal help,
> Possession of the faculties. VII. 623-627.

A furtive nostalgia intrudes, corrupting the lines. For a moment the poet attempts to deal with the city and with nature at once; and then after an honest gesture of helplessness he says:

> But these [spectacles], I fear,
> Are falsely catalogu'd, things that are, are not,
> Even as we give them welcome. VII. 641-643.

And so, having hushed his own natural accent, he concludes with a thought from Coleridge and a rhythm from Shakespeare. More significantly he has to admit that not even the scenes of his own mountain country can gain possession of his faculties without internal help. The fact that they are more welcome than the scenes of the city does not give them a surer power to invade the mind. As for outward things, upon them we may rest the " structures of the mind." But such structures, " Though rear'd upon the base of outward things," are not of that base. They are, rather, " such structures as the mind Builds for itself." The fabric of Salisbury is solidly enough set upon the substantial earth; yet the beauty expressed through that fabric is not of the earth but of that gracious reality which exists only in the creative intelligence. From this intelligence, as Leonardo knew, comes the glory of art, a thousand times more lovely than the earth on which man dwells.

In the first book Wordsworth has exalted eleven lines (490-501) into a rapturous anthem which has to do with the athletic life of his boyhood. He cries out to the " Presences of Nature," to the " Visions of the hills," to the " Souls of lonely places," acknowledging their power and their ministry in forming his mind. Some critics have pondered these lines as suggesting naturalism, and other as manifesting animism. What they do protest is poetic ecstasy. Wordsworth is ascribing to these Presences and Souls the very quality of his own imagination, and he is attributing to them the activities which belong to the plastic power of his mind. He observes that

> The surface of the universal earth
> With triumph, and delight, and hope, and fear,
> Work[s] like a sea. I. 499-501.

Obviously this is poetic ascription. No power outside the mind can cause " The surface of the universal earth " to flow with triumph and delight before the poet's gaze. It is the imagination, the plastic power which softens all things to receive the impress of its hope and fear. Wordsworth here is illustrating that power of ecstatic objectification by which his mind exhalts itself into amazement and worship. " The poetry proceeds, as it ought to do, from the soul of man, communicating its creative energies to the images of the external world."

Before the close of 1800, while he is composing the concluding lines of the second book, Wordsworth is touched by the shadow of that unseen power which moves though unseen among us. He converses " With things that really are," things seen when the bodily eye loses her function, things heard when the fleshly ear forgets her ways. Unapprehendable by the senses, " lost beyond the reach of thought And human knowledge," reality exists for him within the ineffable Being. " Let this be not forgotten," says the poet, " that I still retain'd

> My first creative sensibility,
> That by the regular action of the world
> My soul was unsubdu'd. A plastic power
> Abode with me, a forming hand, at times
> Rebellious, acting in a devious mood,
> A local spirit of its own, at war
> With general tendency, but for the most
> Subservient strictly to the external things
> With which it commun'd. An auxiliar light
> Came from my mind which on the setting sun
> Bestow'd new splendor, the melodious birds,
> The gentle breezes, fountains that ran on,
> Murmuring so sweetly in themselves, obey'd
> A like dominion; and the midnight storm
> Grew darker in the presence of my eye.
> Hence my obeisance, my devotion hence,
> And hence my transport. II. 379-395.

This is not yet clear. But here is a different accent upon what shall become clear. Although the mind seems still to inform itself through the senses, the senses are patently being informed through the mind. Unfortunate as is the term " creative sensibility," we find that the creative power is not subdued by the sensibility. There is recognized something beyond sense, something eternally free of it and above it. The world breaking through cannot quell this thing. For nine times " subservient to external things," on the tenth it rebels and greets them with victory. It grows devious in mood, is centered in itself and imperious. Is the setting sun splendid? It will dash the sun with sempiternal flame. Is the midnight storm dark? The eye of the poet will make the " darkness visible." Dominion, it is dominion that the creative mind must have. The soul of the poet, conscious of its creative energies, rises in transport.

In the four years which passed between the completing of the second book and the beginning of the third, Wordsworth grew in the understanding of his abilities. Since this growth was natural, it was not in a straight line; but it was tortuous. However, as we move forward we find on the whole a clearer treatment of imagination. This clearer treatment might be ascribed to the development of the individual who is being discussed in the poem; but I am inclined to feel that it should be attributed rather to the actual growth of the poet. I make small doubt that had Wordsworth written the first two books in 1804 we should have in them a different babe and a different boy. Surely this " mountain Youth " who now looks out of his window at the statue " Of Newton, with his Prism and silent Face," this " northern Villager " with a strangeness in his mind is far other than a scion of Hartley.

> For hither I had come with holy powers
> And faculties, whether to work or feel:
> To apprehend all passions and all moods
> Which time, and place, and season do impress
> Upon the visible universe, and work
> Like changes there by force of my own mind. III. 83-88.

The similarities existing between this passage and the anthem of the first book are more obvious than is any new quality in the lines. Here the " visible universe " takes the place of the " universal earth "; here the " passions and moods " are akin to " triumph, and delight, and hope, and fear." But here the significant word " work " carries a richer, a more direct and personal meaning. That meaning, furthermore, is immediately associated with the " holy powers " of the poet. No longer are the creative faculties ascribed to " Presences of Nature " alone; they are claimed by the poet himself. We shall appreciate this new emphasis better if we pause briefly to study Wordsworth's use of that word with which he associates the process of creativity.

Some thirteen times in all, while he is writing the *Prelude*,

Wordsworth uses the word " work " rather purely in the sense in which the translators of the authorized version of the Bible used it: " God ended his work "; or, " When I consider the work of thy fingers." When God ended his work he saw that it was good: the void was filled with beauty. This was the supreme act and has become the grand symbol of creativity. Similarly, when the artist ends his work, some beauty exists which before was not. The powers by means of which he accomplishes his work he naturally calls holy. They are, he says, " truly from the Deity." With these things in mind we can discern the fresh quality and the new meaning in the lines we study. The " visible universe " is here, substantial and sure, and it may announce itself to the senses and they may feel it. But upon this universe some high power, indistinctly and inadequately referred to as " time, and place, and season," may impress its moods and passions. And by the holy powers of his own mind the poet may do the same thing.

Perhaps nowhere in the works of Wordsworth does the poetic passion burn with purer flame than it does between lines eighty-two and one hundred ninety-four of the third book. There are grander passages in the *Prelude*; there is no whiter fire. The mature man, as he writes of his experiences at Cambridge, almost achieves the miracle of recapturing the first fine raptures of divine awareness. It is for once as if after-meditation with all its subtle lowerings were cried away. Here is the thing itself.

> O Heavens! how awful is the might of Souls
> And what they do within themselves.   III. 178-179.

Awful incumbencies sweep into the mind: " visitings Of the Upholder of the tranquil Soul." The Creator announces himself to the worker; and as the poet ascends toward highest truth he gives life " To every natural form." He takes the great mass of the world into his being and quickens it.

> I was most rich,
> I had a world about me; 'twas my own,
> I made it; for it only lived to me,
> And to the God who look'd into my mind.   III. 141-144.

Again the high claim and the right claim! The poet makes his own world, a living world, living to him and to the God who knows the life of it; for the life in the work of the worker is the life of the

Creator himself. Call this inspiration, call this prophecy, call it madness—what skills the word? " Of Genius, Power, Creation, Divinity itself I have been speaking," says the poet. " Within my mind I recognize that visionary power which rather makes than finds what it beholds. I have come up now to an eminence, and my mind is now possessed of the shaping spirit of imagination."

As we turn our efforts toward suggesting a definition for imagination, we can do no better than follow the poet's lead and move from the lesser to the greater, from fancy to imagination. By 1815 he had come to an understanding of the distinction between these two terms. He recognized their similarities and their differences. He saw the law with its principle of emphasis which works between them. With a mind unblinded by its own internal lightning, he eschewed the hollow metaphysical jargon which nominates fancy a " mode of memory." He would not split up the mind into a Germanic chaos, but kept the mind a unit working now in this way and now in that. Fancy reaches up ambitiously striving to rival imagination; imagination stoops indulgently to work with the frail materials of fancy. Out of imperceptible similarities all distinctions between them grow through emphasis. Does imagination " aggregate, associate, evoke, and combine "? So, in her way, does fancy. And what is the difference in the way of fancy? That is to ask the difference in the ways of Puck and of Prospero. Fancy is " capricious, playful, ludicrous, tender, or pathetic," and dotes on surprise. She is, indeed, " in her own spirit, a creative faculty "; yet when she has beguiled and quickened the " temporal part of our nature " she is satisfied, and darts away, and lurks among her own pretty fictions. An elvish joyousness is hers; but her light spirit does not concern itself with eternity and truth. These nobler interests she abandons to her elder sister.

It is in the eighth book that we come upon a study of fancy. The poet in later years mulled his lines, spreading through them an anxious dissatisfaction. We may, however, recognize in them a conception similar to that which Wordsworth held in 1815. With characteristic good sense he recognizes that the " first Poetic spirit," that of the " first childhood " and the early years expresses itself in undisciplined fancy, whereas the matured " poetic Faculty," having been disciplined by the hard experiences of life, may express itself through imagination. The child may fancy, but he has not yet the power to imagine; the matured poet, having the greater power, imagination, may also, if he wills, exercise himself in the lesser, fancy.

In Wordsworth's youth he found everything subject to the caprice of "wilful fancy."

> From touch of this new power
> Nothing was safe: the Elder-tree that grew
> Beside the well-known Charnel-house had then
> A dismal look; the Yew-tree had its Ghost,
> That took its station there for ornament:
> Then common death was none, common mishap,
> But matter for this humour everywhere,
> The tragic super-tragic, else left short. VIII. 524-531.

The Widow staggers beneath the blows of her distress; the Annettish Vagrant gathers her Little-ones forlornly beneath some stately Flower. Or does the wet rock glisten in the wood? It is the burnished shield of some Knight suspended over his tomb. No precious bribe could bring the poet to visit the rock; for then actuality would overcome fancy.

> And month by month I saw the spectacle,
> Nor ever once have visited the spot
> Unto this hour. VIII. 580-582.

Even in his maturer years, when he could avoid doing so, Wordsworth visited no Yarrow. "Sight," said he, "is at first a sad enemy of imagination." And as for fancy,—she shuns like death the test of fact. Her nature is anti-empirical. Her penchant is to sport "among the shining streams Of Fairy land." Hers are means which do not "lie in nature," and too often she will not stay within the "limits of experience and of truth." But that she may be purified and learn "to ply her craft By judgment steadied" we may be sure. In proof of her attainment of this better state it is enough to read the second poem to the daisy. The time will come when the fairy shapes of fancy shall be "grafted upon feelings Of the imagination." When the poet learns to replace vagaries with the "real solid world" he is ready for "a time of greater dignity." We may assume that that time has now come, and we may enter now the spacious places of the imperial spirit.

Here we shall live, says Wordsworth, feeling the eternity of life and contemplating "Infinity and God." Spells shall be upon us, and

" Trances of thought and mountings of the mind " shall come upon us. Our souls shall put off their veils and self-transmuted stand as in the presence of their God. " Consummate happiness, wide-spreading, steady, calm, contemplative " shall signal us to rest in this high place where we may not only be " chear'd with stillness " but where we may hear the very breathing of " the immortal Soul." Vows shall be made for us and we shall walk in blessedness.

Unless we are willing to accept this noble language of Wordsworth and to acknowledge his right to these lofty claims, we must miss the essential thing he has to tell us. As did Plato and Plotinus, as do Emerson and Shelley, Wordsworth accepts the interpenetration of the artist's mind by the Creative Intelligence. Man-the-worker creates in virtue of the spirit of God-the-worker which is in him. Standing upon " holy ground " he speaks " no dream but things oracular." As he closes the fifth book Wordsworth considers the " works Of mighty Poets."

> Visionary Power
> Attends upon the motions of the winds
> Embodied in the mystery of words.
> There darkness makes abode, and all the host
> Of shadowy things do work their changes there,
> As in a mansion like their proper home;
> Even forms and substances are circumfused
> By that transparent veil with light divine;
> And through the turnings intricate of Verse,
> Present themselves as objects recognis'd,
> In flashes, and with glory scarce their own. V. 619-629.

The glory is not of the substances and forms; the glory is the prophet-vestment of the soul which comes from God. " Poets, even as Prophets," and together with prophets, because of their awareness of Divinity, are " Connected in a mighty scheme of truth." To them is " vouchsafed An influx "; and Wordsworth trusts that he, as did the poet of Patmos, may " have sight Of a new world "; that he, working at the source of things, may create poetry elemental and true.

This new world, which seems to be of a higher order than that created out of the subtle distinctions and affinities observed in nature, is planet-kin to that other world created by exalted reason out of the pure syntheses of geometric science. Transcendent over sense, working with lucent abstractions, the imagination, as we have already observed, makes at last

> In verity, an independent world
> Created out of pure Intelligence.   VI. 186-187.

Granted that this world is a toy, a plaything, an abstraction delicate as the day-spring fashioned to delight the sense, to bring peace " to a mind beset With images," it nevertheless proves the galaxies. In each star all systems are demonstrated, and Neptune manifests Hercules. By this one hundred and eighty-seventh line we are lifted above confusion. Pure Intelligence is; and Pure Intelligence can fashion out of itself what gleaming shapes it will. Day unto day speaks of this truth, and night unto night shows knowledge of it. So God and the universes are explained; so the poet and his poems.

We have already referred to the imaginative zest with which the young Englishman from the foot of stubby Helvellyn visits the Alps. In his mind these mountains are the cloud-capped and gorgeous monarchs of an ideal world. When he hears the peasant say that he, Wordsworth, has crossed these Alps, the poet is lifted far forward among huge abstractions and is filled with that still agitation which characterizes the imaginative state. More powerfully now than when he was a boy a trouble comes into his mind from unknown causes; in sudden strength his mind begins to work with " unknown modes of being." Now, as formerly, there is the sense of blank desertion, of being " left alone, Seeking the visible world." But now, while the visible world is lost, the invisible is suddenly revealed.

> Imagination! lifting up itself
> Before the eye and progress of my Song
> Like an unfather'd vapour; here that Power,
> In all the might of its endowments, came
> Athwart me; I was lost as in a cloud,
> Halted, without a struggle to break through.
> And now recovering, to my Soul I say
> I recognise thy glory; in such strength
> Of usurpation, in such visitings
> Of awful promise, when the light of sense
> Goes out in flashes that have shewn to us
> The invisible world, doth Greatness make abode,
> There harbours whether we be young or old.
> Our destiny, our nature, and our home
> Is with infinitude, and only there.   VI. 525-539.

These lines usher in the familiar visionary state, a state of rapture and of revelation. The Alps are suddenly lost away, the intelligence is utterly free in its workings, and the poet enters his

own world, the invisible, there to participate in the Imperial Greatness, there with infinitude to make his home. To such a man
as Wordsworth this experience is of deepest consequence. The
aesthetic is completed in the spiritual: beauty is transmuted into
truth. Must we anticipate the later changes of his mind toward the
formally religious? Here, then we must begin. The intelligence
that has known the Infinite may well repose. And Wordsworth's
imaginative wisdom has brought him to the very center of infinity.

> The unfetter'd clouds, and region of the Heavens,
> Tumult and peace, the darkness and the light
> Were all like workings of one mind, the features
> Of the same face, blossoms upon one tree,
> Characters of the great Apocalypse,
> The types and symbols of Eternity,
> Of first and last, and midst, and without end.   VI. 566-572.

Here is a mighty conception of the unity of Mind. The ecstatic
synthesis has been achieved. The power we study has gathered
everything within itself and lost it all in Eternity.

We began our study of Wordsworth who, poet though he was, for
a time allowed his intelligence to be imposed upon and oppressed by
recurrent suggestions of sensism. We paused with him while he
learned that

> Truth is within ourselves; it takes no rise
> From outward things, whate'er you may believe.
> There is an inmost center in us all,
> Where truth abides in fulness; and around,
> Wall upon wall, the gross flesh hems it in,
> This perfect, clear perception—which is truth.
> A baffling and perverting carnal mesh
> Binds it, and makes all error: and, to KNOW,
> Rather consists in opening out a way
> Whence the imprisoned splendor may escape,
> Than in effecting entry for a light
> Supposed to be without.   *Paracelsus,* I.

We have now come with him to the place where he stands sure, participating in " The Soul, the Imagination of the whole." Splendors
are within him, but they are not imprisoned. They pass freely into
the light that is without, and freely the light passes into the place
of the splendors. There is no place where man the effect ceases and
where God the cause begins. All is a majestic intellect feeding upon

infinity. Awareness of this truth is " the highest bliss That can
be known " by a poet. Through this awareness he gains the consciousness of who he is—one truly from the Deity. And the power
within him and within the Deity, the power which gives him his
consummate assurance, is

> Imagination, which, in truth,
> Is but another name for absolute strength
> And clearest insight, amplitude of mind,
> And reason in her most exalted mood. XIII. 167-170.

University of Michigan.

WORDSWORTH: THE PROPERTY OF FORTITUDE

By Bennett Weaver

" It is the property of fortitude not to be easily terrified by the dread of things pertaining to death; to possess good confidence in things terrible, and presence of mind in dangers. . . . Moreover, it is the property of fortitude to labor and endure."—Aristotle's " Synopsis of the Virtues and Vices," Vol. IX, p. 395, ed. Bekker. Quoted by Wordsworth to Beaumont, March 12, 1805.

I

Students of Wordsworth have persistently differed in their understanding of his treatment of virtue and evil, of joy and pain. I have little doubt that these differences arise from what Andrew Chester Bradley calls " a disproportionate emphasis on certain aspects of his mind and writings." [1] Since in the judgment of some readers the conclusions of this paper may be vitiated by such over-emphasis, I wish to state that I am at least aware of the danger. Further, I would record the fact that not only Wordsworth himself but Matthew Arnold, his sufficient apologist, and many others have placed great stress upon the " healing power " of joy in the poems we shall read. In their way, paradoxically they speak somewhat on the side of those against whom I must contend. For where the one group charges the poet with a neglect of the evil and pain in life, the other cries him up for his moral power and his deep joyousness. I wish to take a position more directly against his accusers and, indeed, obligate myself to do no more than readjust what appear to me to be certain of their disproportionate emphases.

William Hazlitt, whom Wordsworth regarded as " a man of extraordinary acuteness, but perverse as Lord Byron himself," [2] spoke with sharp accent of what he thought to be the lack of honesty and fortitude in the poet.

He calms the throbbing pulses of his heart, by keeping his eyes ever fixed on the face of nature. . . . No storm, no shipwreck startles us by its horrors: but the rainbow lifts its head in the cloud. . . . No sad vicissitude of fate, no overwhelming catastrophe in nature deforms his

---

[1] Andrew Chester Bradley, *Oxford Lectures on Poetry* (London: Macmillan, 1919), p. 100.

[2] Alexander B. Grosart, *The Prose Works of William Wordsworth* (London: Edward Moxon, 1876), III, 262.

page: but the dew-drop glitters on the bending flower, the tear collects in the glistening eye.[3]

He is a man, concludes Hazlitt, "having no unruly and violent passions"; he is indeed a "spoiled child."

Professor Benjamin Putnam Kurtz, in *The Pursuit of Death,* recalls the accusations of Hazlitt and insists, as did the older critic, that Wordsworth "was not thoroughly candid in facing the facts of life."

Perhaps it was this early disinclination and neglect vividly to envisage death as the possible failure of all human endeavour, that gave to Words-worth's mature poetry both its special power to impart a healing peace to some troubled but not too critical minds, and its curious insufficiency for other minds more thoroughly critical. For it may be held that the amazing self-confidence of the poet of *Tintern Abbey* and *The Prelude* was attained at the expense of neglecting some of the obvious facts of experience. Retreating in dismay from the tragic sense of life that the French Revolution stirred in him, he too easily found refuge by reassuming the rather uncritical peace of mind he had known in this adolescent intercourse with nature. Hazlitt believed that he was not thoroughly candid in facing the facts of life. It is difficult to defend him against that indictment. . . . The possibility of a malignant, or at least neutral, uni-verse he almost deliberately understated. The desolation of war and death is heard afar, its clamour muted to "the still, sad music of humanity." The "burden of the mystery," "the weary weight of all this unintelligible world," is lightened too readily by the "serene and blessed" mood of the mystic. . . . Had his earliest communings with nature in its serene aspects been rudely shocked by its other aspect of internecine murder, his later ministry of peace might have been more thoughtful and powerful. Per-haps, too, in a keener struggle he would have lost the complacency of self-sanctified dullness which spreads through the huge mass of his inferior work. But, in a way, when one is born, one is done for.[4]

The indictment is clear, and it is a grave indictment. If beneath the surface of the "tranquil life" which Legouis ascribes to Words-worth[5] there are lodged cowardly and uncandid repressions, then

---

[3] William Hazlitt, *The Spirit of the Age* (London and New York: "Everymans," 1925), pp. 252-254. Cf. *My First Acquaintance with Poets:* "There was a severe, worn pressure of thought about his temples."

[4] Benjamin Putnam Kurtz, *The Pursuit of Death* (New York, 1933), pp. 72-73.

[5] Émile Hyacinthe Legouis, *The Early Life of William Wordsworth* (London and Toronto, 1921), p. 466: "It is not a procreative nature of which he sings. Neither is it the nature which destroys. He found that conception . . . among the fair hills of Cumberland [cf. *The Brothers,*

we can no longer deal with the poet in good faith. We must join with Herbert Read; [6] and where Arnold finds a " profound genuineness," a " powerful and beautiful application of ideas to life," [7] we must expect evasion and childish frailty. We must anticipate that the poet, having smothered the truth about certain facts in his private life,[8] will suppress the truth about life itself. He will come at last to the " decolorated and frigescent world " in which Garrod finds him in 1807.[9]

II

Since the charge does not concern itself purely with literary criticism but involves the facts of Wordsworth's life, we must scrutinize those facts. Is the poet indeed one whose sternest experience was basking " in the sun of a summer's day "? Is he one who suffers from " an early disinclination and neglect vividly to envisage death? " The answer is ready.

> Early died
> My honour'd Mother; she who was the heart
> And hinge of all our learnings and our loves:

ll. 364-382, and *George and Sarah Green*, ed. by E. de Selincourt, Oxford, 1936], where no avalanche nor wild animal is to be dreaded . . . where slumber lakes innocent [cf. Brothers Water and the tale 'of William Watson and of Mary Watson whose " end was more tragical than that of the young man " drowned in Grasmere. Pp. 89-91 of Dorothy Wordsworth's ms. as published by de Selincourt]. What a happy result of narrowness of vision! " Cf. note 22 *infra*, among others suggested to me by Professor Arthur Palmer Hudson.

[6] Herbert E. Read, *Wordsworth*, The Clark Lectures, 1929-1930 (London, 1930), pp. 103-135.

[7] Matthew Arnold, *Essays in Criticism* (New York, n. d.), p. 353.

[8] Willard L. Sperry, *Wordsworth's Anti-Climax* (Cambridge, 1935), p. 80: " It is to the poet's credit that he never hid the truth from his near of kin and his friends—Dorothy, Mary, Coleridge, Francis Wrangham, the Clarksons, the Montagus, Crabb Robinson, Quillinan, Miss Fenwick, Caroline, Baduin, Christopher Wordsworth."

[9] Heathcote William Garrod, *Wordsworth* (Oxford, 1927), p. 122. Here, too, as Professor Hudson has pointed out to me, we might remember DeQuincey's remark in *Tait's Edinburgh Magazine* for January, 1839, Volume VI, p. 9: " The nose,, a little arched and large . . . has always been accounted an unequivocal expression of animal appetites organically strong. And that was in fact the basis of Wordsworth's intellectual power: his intellectual passions were fervent and strong; because they rested upon a basis of animal sensibility superior to that of most men, diffused through *all* the animal passions."

> She left us destitute, and as we might
> Trooping together. Little suits it me
> To break upon the sabbath of her rest.
> .   .   .   .   .   .   She was pure
> From feverish dread of error and mishap
> And evil.   *The Prelude*, V, 256-278.

In these restrained lines we recognize a woman who had in her nature the fortitude which Aristotle describes. Being pure from the " feverish dread of evil," she was, like the Greek, ' 'not easily terrified by the dread of things." What the son may have inherited from the mother we need not conjecture; but we do observe that he described some of her characteristics almost in the words of Aristotle. And when this mother died her son was eight years old. " The premature loss of such a guardian is a misfortune rarely, if ever, to be repaired," an anonymous biographer of Cowper quotes another as saying. In the midst of a long attestation to the truth of the statement he himself remarks: " Nor do we here lay too much stress on the feelings of a child, whether regarded in themselves or in the inferences to be thence educed." [10] With this point of view Horace E. Scudder is in sympathy, attaching significance to the death of Keats's mother while " He was still a boy," and observing that " he grieved for her with the force of a passionate nature." [11] This sense of grief and of desolation is so common to bereaved children that we must assume it affected Wordsworth unless particular proof of his abnormality be offered and unless the evidence we have be controverted.

When the boy was thirteen years of age his father died. The family was broken up. There were often enough days when misery clung to the hearts of the children, separated as they were from one another. In four years, however, the boy was at Cambridge; and at the age of eighteen, being in London, he began to see the world.

> What a hell
> For eyes and ears! what anarchy and din
> Barbarian and infernal! 'tis a dream,
> Monstrous in colour, motion, shape, sight, sound.
>   *The Prelude*, VII, 658-661.

------

[10] *The Poetical Works of William Cowper* (London: T. Nelson and Sons, 1859), pp. xii-xiii.

[11] Horace E. Scudder, *The Complete Poetical Works and Letters of John Keats* (Boston and New York: Houghton Mifflin, 1899), p. xv.

At twenty he was tramping through France, Switzerland, and Italy—an experience men have strained to evaluate in Chaucer, thrilled to suggest for Shakespeare, and paused to measure for Milton. At twenty-one he was in the France of the Revolution; and at twenty-two he was fleeing to preserve his life, having left behind him Annette and the baby Caroline.[12]

Up to this point it is difficult to see how one with justice may speak of Wordsworth's " clear and tranquil life." It is hard to find here the beginnings of " self-sanctified dullness," or to draw from the record of these years critical justification for the remark that " in a way, when one is born, one is done for." It is impossible to see the application of Hazlitt's phrase, " having no unruly and violent passions." Far the easiest thing is to credit what Wordsworth said of himself in 1847: " An intimate friend of hers [his mother] . . . told me that she once said to her, that the only one of her five children about whose future she was anxious, was William; and he, she said, would be remarkable either for good or for evil. The cause was, that I was of a stiff, moody, and violent temper." [13]

When, in the October of 1792, Wordsworth returned from France he believed passionately in the principles of the Republic. In less than a year England declared war upon France. The young republican became a wanderer in his own land, thrown out of the pale of love, his sentiments " Sour'd and corrupted upwards to the source." While Blake sang his *Songs of Experience* Wordsworth brooded upon *Guilt and Sorrow*. The theme of the deserted mother fastened upon his mind. His philosophy whirled and blackened and changed. Then death came again into his life, but death vicarious with the gift of freedom. Raisley Calvert left his friend 900 pounds. The test was come.

However, before we observe whether or not Wordsworth used the experiences of these stiff, moody, and violent years, and made poetry out of them, we must follow a little further the record of his life. For three years subsequent to the death of Calvert the poet lived at Racedown and at Alfoxden. He met Coleridge. In the September

---

[12] At this point we may recall the evidence offered by George McLean Harper (*Quarterly Review*, CCXLVIII, April, 1927; *LTLS*, May 1, 1930) that Wordsworth " defied the guillotine " to see Annette Vallon in 1793.

[13] Alexander B. Grosart, *op. cit.*, p. 220.

of 1798 he joined with his friend in the publication of the *Lyrical Ballads*. During the following winter he lived in Germany, continuing there his work on the *Prelude*. By 1802 Wordsworth had decided not to wed Annette Vallon, choosing rather Mary Hutchinson. Before making this decision, with what may have been an unusual candor and courage, he spent four weeks with Annette and their daughter Caroline. In the next seven years five more children were born to him; and in the year when he finished his master work, his beloved brother John was drowned.

"No storm, no shipwreck startles us with its horrors," says Hazlitt.

> Sea—Ship—drowned—Shipwreck—so it came,
> The meek, the brave, the good, was gone;
> He who had been our living John
> Was nothing but a name. *Elegiac Verses*, 37-40.

Long as the mighty rocks endure let these words stand, says the poet:

> Oh do not Thou too fondly brood,
> Although deserving of all good,
> On any earthly hope, however pure. *Ibid.*, 68-70.

"Poor William was overcome on Saturday—and with floods of tears wrote those verses," Dorothy wrote to Lady Beaumont on June 11th.[14] But Hazlitt had been dead fifteen years before the verses were published, and through death wins an extenuation which cannot readily be granted to his followers in the practice of imputing to Wordsworth a "neglect vividly to envisage death as the possible failure of all human endeavor." Hazlitt never heard this cry of "Unutterable woe." Neither did he know the words written twenty-three years later, words which might well have been addressed to him:

> To life, to *life* give back thine ear:
> Ye who are longing to be rid
> Of fable, though to truth subservient, hear
> The little sprinkling of cold earth that fell
> Echoed from the coffin-lid;
> The convict's summons in the steeple's knell;
> 'The vain distress gun,' from a leeward shore,
> Repeated—heard, and heard no more! [15]
>
> *On the Power of Sound*, 153-160.

---

[14] Ernest de Selincourt, *Dorothy Wordsworth* (Oxford, 1933), p. 194.

[15] These lines haunted Henry Reed "for not a little while." See Leslie Nathan Broughton, *Wordsworth and Reed* (Ithaca, 1933), p. 69.

For nearly a quarter of a century the sound of this distress gun echoed in the mind of Wordsworth. The poem of 1828 phrases once more the letter of March 12, 1805, which the author sent to Sir George Beaumont: " She struck at 5 p. m.　Guns were fired immediately, and were continued to be fired." [16]　Had Hazlitt known the record he must have refrained from his sarcastic reference to glistening tears.　Surely had he read Wordsworth's letter of " Tuesday Evening," 1805. his manhood would have corrected him: " We weep much to-day, and that relieves us.　As to fortitude, I hope I shall show that, and that all of us will show it in a proper time, in keeping down many a silent pang hereafter. . . . And yet, what virtue and what goodness, what heroism and courage, what triumphs of disinterested love everywhere, and human life, after all, what is it ! " [17]

Although Hazlitt did not know these poems and letters charged with the bitter contemplation of the " possible failure of all human endeavour " no matter how virtuous or heroic, he should have known the *Elegiac Stanzas*.　Why did he not say, " It is an honest poem "?　He knew his Shakespeare well; he knew the o'er-fraught heart and the heart whose low sounds reverb'd no hollowness.　When Wordsworth, remembering the fatal fifth of February, 1805, wrote: " The feeling of my loss will ne'er be old; A power is gone, which nothing can restore," why did not the acute critic observe that " His absent Brother still was at his heart "?　And why did he venture no sympathetic comment on the strange fact that it was close to the February of 1805 that Wordsworth seems to pass the peak of his poetic power?

In 1812 Wordsworth again meets death.　He writes to Archbishop Wrangham: " I have lost two sweet children, a boy and a girl, at the ages of four and six and a half.　These innocents were the delight of our hearts.　They were cut off in a few hours—one by the measles, and the other by convulsions." [18]　It is possibly after this experience that the poet who has, we are told, not been " shocked by internecine murder " in Nature writes the lines entitled *Maternal Grief*.

[16] Alexander B. Grosart, *op. cit.*, p. 249.
[17] *Ibid.*, p. 250.
[18] Alexander B. Grosart, *op. cit.*, p. 264.

> Such union, in the lovely Girl maintained
> And her twin Brother, had the parent seen,
> Ere, pouncing like a ravenous bird of prey,
> Death in a moment parted them.   38-41.[19]

Beyond his forty-second year the poet's life was often burdened with pain and grief. He had no need to pursue death; for death pursued him. Calamity invaded the thinning group of those who were dear to him. The hand of the poet was practised in epitaphs and elegiac pieces. Death took his near friends; death took his grandchild, " as noble a boy as ever was seen "; and when he was old death took his daughter Dora. Ellis Yarnell found " The expression of his countenance sad, mournful; he seemed one on whom sorrow pressed heavily." [20] Perhaps more severe than the pain caused by these things was the long uncertainty occasioned by the condition of his sister Dorothy. " Thy mind shall be a mansion for all lovely forms," he had said in the days of their glory; but the later days had wrecked the mansion. If, in short, there is anything unusual about the facts of Wordsworth's life it is to be found in the passionate nature of the early years, in the noble accomplishment of the great years, and in the quality of that fortitude with which he met the common inevitabilities of the later days.

III

Doomed as all men are " to go in company with Pain, And Fear " Wordsworth learned to take the shocks of life with honor. However, the charge is not so much against his life as against his page. Granted that his life was reasonably similar to that of other men, yet, we are told, " No sad vicissitude of fate, no overwhelming catastrophe in nature deforms his page." His page is complacent.

It is, then, his page which we must examine. Since obviously we cannot scrutinize all of his poems, we shall select those of the characteristic and sufficient decade of 1795-1805.[21] Within these ten years it should be incredible that we might evade the issue. If

---

[19] *Ibid.* See Fenwick note no. 68, p. 25: " This is faithfully set forth from my wife's feelings and habits after the loss of our two children." These lines, then, must have been written sometime after December 1, 1812, not in 1810 as has usually been stated.

[20] Alexander B. Grosart, *op. cit.*, p. 478.

[21] Edith C. Batho, *The Later Wordsworth* (Cambridge, 1933).

in a later period his passion, " fervent as it was," has suffered change, we shall say with him:

> How could there fail to be
> Some change, if merely hence, that years of life
> Were going on, and with them loss or gain
> Inevitable, sure alternative.   *The Prelude*, XI, 38-41.

Against the odd accusation that " no overwhelming catastrophe in nature deforms his page," let the poet of 1804 speak.

> Thou also, Man, hast wrought,
> For commerce of thy nature with itself,
> Things worthy of unconquerable life;
> And yet we feel, we cannot chuse but feel
> That these must perish. Tremblings of the heart
> It gives, to think that the immortal being
> No more shall need such garments; and yet Man,
> As long as he shall be the Child of Earth,
> Might almost ' weep to have ' what he may lose,
> Nor be himself extinguish'd; but survive
> Abject, depress'd, forlorn, disconsolate.
> A thought is with me sometimes, and I say,
> Should earth by inward throes be wrench'd throughout,
> Or fire be sent from far to wither all
> Her pleasant habitations, and dry up
> Old Ocean in his bed left sing'd and bare, . . .
> Yea, all the adamantine holds of truth, . . .
> Where would they be?   *The Prelude*, V, 17-44.

From these speculations the poet wakes in terror.

Against the charge of complacency and of self-sanctified dullness we place a brief statement of Wordsworth's purpose. That purpose is to deal with the real passions of men. The " elemental feelings " working under " the primary laws of our nature " are his theme. The capricious and the arbitrary are to be neglected; the essential is to be expressed. The poet is to look steadily on human life and to give artistic interpretation to what he sees. If ultimately he is to subdue " melancholy Fear " by Faith, he is nevertheless " intent to weigh the good and evil of our mortal state."

We turn, then, to the *Lyrical Ballads*; for surely in *Guilt and Sorrow* Wordsworth has not neglected " unruly and violent passions "; and surely in *The Borderers,* as he himself states, he treats " this awful truth; that as . . . sin and crime are apt to start from their very opposite qualities, so are there no limits to the

hardening of the heart and the perversion of the understanding."
Almost all of Wordsworth's Ballads are about real people; and they
are marked by that rare quality of the real which characterizes the
best of the old ballads. There is in them little evidence of what
might with any exactness be called calming the throbbings of the
heart by keeping the " eye ever fixed on the face of nature." The
range of the poems is not great; but they have the stamp of integrity
upon them. Among them none is more highly charged with emo-
tional truth than the pieces dealing with the deserted mother and
child. The story of *The Thorn* is typical, and it is not sanctified:
A woman who loves and who is promised marriage is deserted for
another woman. Like Ruth, she goes mad, and fearfully carouses
her cup of wrong. She murders her child, dons " a scarlet cloak,"
and " At all times of the day and night " watches near the grave.
The whole situation is full of misery and horror. And the man?
He is described in the more familiar poem *Ruth*—perchance the
poet himself hidden in a psychic light?

> With hues of genius on his cheek
> In finest tones the Youth could speak:
> —While he was yet a boy,
> The moon, the glory of the sun,
> And streams that murmur as they run,
> Had been his dearest joy. . . .
>
> The wind, the tempest roaring high,
> The tumult of a tropic sky,
> Might well be dangerous food
> For him, a Youth to whom was given
> So much of earth—so much of heaven,
> And such impetutous blood.

A man " having no unruly and violent passions," says the critic.
" He," said Wordsworth's mother, " would be remarkable either for
good or for evil."

Among the *Lyrical Ballads* there is also the weird and ghastly
story of Goody Blake and Harry Gill. One must be insensitive to
the stark quality of poetry if having read this story of an old woman
living alone on the northern side of a hill, poor with a terrible
poverty, he can say that it has little to do with the desolation of
life. And what but starkness, crude and deceptive, can keep one
from finding in *Simon Lee* a profound misery? Could not Wordsworth have said to Simon: " Nay, and thou too, old man, in former

days wast, as we hear, happy"? Maugre the matter of the artistry involved, is it not just that which our poet does say? For Simon in former days had the strength to outrun horses. Now he is little and lean and sick.

> Oh the heavy change!—bereft
> Of health, strength, friends, and kindred,

he bows down in the "second twilight." Is not this the change which Lear felt, although with another intensity, as he looked back upon the days when with his "good biting falcion" he made them skip? But Wordsworth does not write of an old king begging the body of his son, of an old king staggering forward with the body of his daughter. His art is to select the least of the things which broken age cannot do, the very least: it cannot cut the root of a tree. By this means he would make us know "the heavy change." He catches in the instant the pathetic powerlessness of age, and hints to us that to this image we must all come.

> O Man, that from thy fair and shining youth
> Age might but take the things Youth needed not!

To what Matthew Arnold calls the "bare, sheer penetrating power" of Wordsworth responses naturally differ. But to the poignancy of *The Last of the Flock* Hazlitt himself might well say: "No one has displayed the same pathos in treating the simplest feelings of the heart." However, we must omit further comment on the shorter Ballads in order to examine the lines composed above Tintern Abbey. It is in these lines that Professor Kurtz finds "The desolation of war and death . . . muted to 'the still, sad music of humanity.'" He should first of all have finished the sentence: "Nor harsh nor grating, though of ample power To chasten and subdue." What more should be demanded? Is it the property of fortitude to harass itself with a greater harshness than is needed to chasten the spirit? Is it the function of art to deal with the pain of life in an uncontrolled manner? The *Letter to the Bishop of Landaff* then should serve if we must have the loud and the passionate. But is it not enough to carry into the lovely haunts of the Wye a sense of "the heavy and the weary weight of All this unintelligible world"? Shall not a poet be thought of as more than a man dismayed if, remebering the "evil tongues, Rash judgments, the sneers of selfish men," he turn toward peace in the presence of beauty?

Of the four poems written in 1798 but not published in the *Lyrical Ballads,* two are short descriptive pieces, one a development of the theme of *Animal Tranquility and Decay,* and the other is *Peter Bell.* This last poem has in it 890 lines more than the other three combined; and during the twenty-one years it remained in manuscript Wordsworth took pains "to make the production less unworthy." Admitting that "the habits, tricks, and physiognomy of asses " may not delight us as greatly as they did the poet, what, nevertheless, is the poem about? Briefly this: Peter Bell, the potter, is a wild, cunning, hard, and impudent man. Already having ten wives he yet lures away a sixteen year old girl, virtually to become her murderer and the murderer of her unborn child of sorrow, Benoni. In his night wanderings Peter comes upon an ass gazing into a moonlit stream, and thinks to steal the creature. Suddenly, however, he sees the face of the owner of the ass, a ghastly face glittering against the moon in the water. This cracks the ice away from Peter's imagination,

> And, after ten month's melancholy [he]
> Became a good and honest man.

We may suspect the sudden repentance of Peter; we may revolt at his sentimentalism; and we may accuse him directly of " a religious ' retreat.' " But surely in the story of Peter's life sufficient evil has been recognized.

The dominant theme of the poems of 1799 is death. *There was a Boy* treats the theme with the intimacy of self-identification. On summer evenings when his way led through the church-yard, the poet says,

> A long half-hour together I have stood
> Mute—looking at the grave in which he lies!

In this year also Wordsworth writes the "Lucy Poems"; and whether, as Coleridge thinks, they deal in fancy with " the moment in which his sister should die," or whether they are fictive, they contain poetry which Aubrey de Vere recognizes as " impassioned beyond the comprehension of those who fancy that Wordsworth lacks passion, merely because in him passion is neither declamatory, nor, latently, sensual."

Following the pagination of the Cambridge edition of the poet's works, we pass next through *A Poet's Epitaph,* the title of which is a sufficient comment, to the *Address to the Scholars of the Village School of* ——. When he wrote this poem he could not have had out of his mind Gray's *Ode on a Distant Prospect of Eton College.* The "little noisy Crew" of Wordsworth's mournful *Address* is recruited from the "little victims" of the head master of the grave-yard school. Immediately following this dirge are the "Matthew Poems," studies which in themselves celebrate chiefly a dead man's reaction to the death of his child.

> Poor Matthew, all his frolics o'er,
> Is silent as a standing pool.

And the poet remembers when this dear paradoxical fellow turned from his daughter's grave only to come upon a fair child "whose hair was wet With points of morning dew." So pierced with long-ing was this man that he could not wish the child his own. In the third poem of the group, above the

> witty rhymes
> About the crazy old church-clock,
> And the bewildered chimes,

we hear this tolling paradox :

> The wiser mind
> Mourns less for what age takes away
> Than what it leaves behind.

And what for this Happy Warrior is the end? His own name upon his place of death!

Directly we leave Matthew we come upon a sexton with a wheel-barrow full of bones, finger joints and skulls to be piled in the bone-house. As we turn from the ghastly fellow we are confronted by a sweet-faced idiot, the Danish boy. "Like a dead Boy he is serene." Immediately beyond him is Lucy Gray,

> The sweetest thing that ever grew
> Beside a human door.

But what are we told of this sweetest thing? In language pure and poignant we are told that lost among the careless powers of nature she is killed. What avails? Still beyond her is another figure of pain, Ruth, crazed with betrayal, fleeing from the madhouse to play until death with "the engines of her pain." The best she can hope for in life is the alleviation which idiocy brings her; the last she can expect in death is that her body shall lie "in hallowed mould." The poems of 1799 close with such a poem to a fly as Uncle Toby might have written for Corporal Trim. It is a strange year; and one on the whole given to the pursuit of death.

We may not continue to particularize; and yet in an eclectic treatment of the work of the next five years we find no need to vary the course of our investigation. Although the subject matter of the poems becomes more diverse and although a raw chill invades less the whole body of them, yet the brooding upon sin, desertion, old age, and death continues; and at the end of the half decade we come full upon the disaster of Wordsworth's mature years, the death of his brother John. The great poem of 1800 is *Michael*, which was "founded on the son of an old couple having become dissolute and run away from his parents." The theme has been reputable since the days of David. Our greatest English tragedy considers "How sharper than a serpent's tooth it is to have a thankless child." Yet I find that the real burden of *Michael* is something heavier than this. It is the necessitous defeat of man, the defeat rendering his noblest heroism a portion of the eternal nothing. The very measure of his courage is the measure of his defeat. No vaunting here of a head that is bloody but unbowed. Man goeth to his long home, and there is no mourner to go about the street.

> **The remains**
> Of the unfinished Sheepfold may be seen;

and as for the rest—

> The ploughshare has been through the ground.

Passing the barren year of 1801 [22] we come to the time of the flower poems and the lines celebrating the rainbow. Yet no critic would turn to these poems for the dominant mood of the year any more than he would quote *The Redbreast chasing the Butterfly* to prove that the poet's world of nature was "red in tooth" and man

---

[22] On Wednesday, December 23, 1801, Dorothy wrote in her *Journal:* "William worked at *The Ruined Cottage* and made himself very ill. . . . A broken soldier came to beg . . . Afterwards a tall woman."—Legouis who, "in a moral sense" does not find the work Wordsworthian, yet says: "He was a great poet when, in 1797, he wrote *The Ruined Cottage.* . . . In itself, the tale is most distressing and desolate. Wordsworth's usual optimism is not to be found in it." (*CHEL*, Vol. XI, 121.)

himself a creature "with vile claws (*The Prelude*, IV, 302)." As a matter of fact, there is this illuminating entry in Dorothy's *Journal* for Tuesday, February 2nd: " After tea I read aloud the eleventh book of *Paradise Lost*. We were much impressed." If we may infer from a conscious paraphrase in *The Redbreast,*

> Could Father Adam open his eyes
> And see this sight beneath the skies,
> He'd wish to close them again,

they were most impressed by the sights which Adam saw. "Alas," cried Adam, as he saw Abel " Rowling in dust and gore, . . .

> But have I now seen Death? Is this the way
> I must return to native dust? O sight
> Of terror, foul and ugly to behold,
> Horrid to think, how horrible to feel! "
>   To whom thus Michael:—" Death thou hast seen
> In his first shape on man; but many shapes
> Of Death . . .
> Before thee shall appear."   *Paradise Lost*, XI, 462-475.

And within a lazar house guarded by the monster with the dart Adam saw

> Numbers of all diseas'd—all maladies
> Of ghastly Spasm, or racking torture, qualmes
> Of heart-sick Agonie, all feavorous kinds,
> Convulsions, Epilepsies, fierce Catarrhs,
> Intestin Stone and Ulcer, Colic pangs,
> Dropsies, and Asthma's, and Joint-racking Rheums.
>   *Ibid.*, ll. 480-485.

However, the marked thinking of 1802 went into the sonnets, many of which speak against Hazlitt with " a voice whose sound is like the sea." When a man shakes a nation with song it is no time to talk of dewdrops glittering on slender flowers.

Aside from the sonnets, furthermore, the most characteristic poem of the year is *Resolution and Independence*. Let us observe some of the materials which went into this work. Dorothy tells us: " We met an old man almost double. He had had a wife, and ' she was a good woman, and it pleased God to bless us with ten children.' All of these were dead but one, of whom he had not heard for many years. He had been hurt in driving a cart, his leg broken, his body driven over, his skull fractured." From such materials as these

Wordsworth builds a noble study in fortitude. There is no dismay at life in this triumphant man. " In his extreme old age " he keeps a firm mind; and when he says, " Still I persevere," the words rebuke all moody cowardice. If suffering is to be absorbed into strength and if the " sad vicissitudes of fate " are to be transmuted into resoluteness, this poem does not fail. The study of the emigrant mother has tenderness in it; the study of the sailor's mother has even greater tenderness; but the great work of the year has power.

Just as among the poems of 1800 *Michael* stands out and among those of 1802 the sonnets and *Resolution and Independence* are preeminent, so among those of 1803 *Yew Trees* and the " Burns Poems " hold a dominant place. In the first of these Coleridge found " imaginative power " comparable to that of Shakespeare and Milton, and Ruskin found a forrest landscape " the most vigorous and solemn ever painted." [23] And what is it that we see among the up-coiling trunks? "Ghostly Shapes—Fear and trembling Hope, Silence and Foresight; Death the Skeleton And Time the Shadow." What a comment, also, upon Hazlitt are the first verses of the poem *At the Grave of Burns*:

> I shiver, Spirit fierce and bold,
> At thought of what I now behold.

For Wordsworth there were no rainbows over the grotesque churchyard at Dumfries. We know that his reflections there were " melancholy and painful "; and we know the very words he and his sister spoke over the grave, the words of " The poor Inhabitant below "— one who has never been accused of being a " spoiled child " or of indulging in " self-sanctified dullness."

We pass into the year 1804, a year made memorable by *To the Cuckoo,* " She was a Phantom of delight," " I wandered lonely as a cloud," and *The Small Celandine*. Yet here also are the seven sisters of Binnorie who leap to death to escape the Sabine woe, here is the bitterly afflicted Margaret, living in a world of " troubles beyond relief," and crying out,

> 'T is falsely said
> That there was ever intercourse
> Between the living and the dead.

---

[23] Andrew J. George, *The Complete Poetical Works of William Wordsworth* (Boston and New York: Houghton Mifflin, 1904), p. 848.

Here also are the arresting lines which are called " an overflow "
from the preceding poem, " preserved in the faint hope that [they]
may turn to account by restoring a shy lover to some forsaken
damsel." Without at all making a point of the matter, may I venture to suggest that we think of William and Annette as we read the
lines, and of William most?

> The peace which others seek they find;
> The heaviest storms not longest last;
> Heaven grants even to the guiltiest mind
> An amnesty for what is past;
> When will my sentence be reversed?
> I only pray to know the worst;
> And wish, as if my heart would burst.
>
> O weary struggle! silent years
> Tell seemingly no doubtful tale;
> And yet they leave it short, and fears
> And hopes are strong and will prevail.
> My calmest faith escapes not pain;
> And, feeling that the hope is vain,
> I think that he will come again.

If these lines were in all honesty intended to restore some " shy
lover to some forsaken damsel," it may have been well that they
were not printed until 1845. Annette died in 1841.

It is in 1805 that we find the only poem of Wordsworth's which
Matthew Arnold could not read with pleasure, *Vaudracour and
Julia*. Nevertheless, it is an important poem; and what the
Victorian critic might have thought of it had he found it an integral
part of the record of the growth of the poet's mind it is interesting
to speculate. But to leave speculation and to return to our theme:
If this poem records " no unruly and violent passions " then what
is it that it does record? Its accompanying piece, the *Ode to Duty*,
is of similar quality. One might call the work a very *tour de force*
of defeat. But if one ask, What lies back of this yearning " for a
repose that ever is the same," the poem confesses itself. The mood
that deeply marks this year is that of inconsolable grief over the
death of John. " No shipwreck startles us by its horrors," wrote
Hazlitt. " Sea—Ship—drowned—Shipwreck," wrote Wordsworth.

IV

Back of all these shorter poems, like a mountain range against which foothills lift their heads and shoulders, lies the *Prelude*. To the student of Wordsworth's thought it is his most difficult and most treacherous work, difficult because of its ascent to where "the heaven of heavens is but a veil," treacherous because of the author's unwillingness "to submit the poetic spirit to the chains of fact and real circumstance." We enter the poem through a burst of transport. Some "heavy weight" has been lifted off this mind. Among "Trances of thought" and a tempest of creative energies a voice shouts: "I am free to drink wild water!" The weary days that were not made for the poet are past; "The holy life of music and of verse" is come.

In his "Earliest cummunings with nature," says Professor Kurtz, Wordsworth was not "shocked by internecine murder." I do not know what exclusive interpretation should in fairness be given to the word "internecine" as it is used here; but the fact of the matter is that in his early years the poet moved among the creatures of nature himself the murderer. It is one thing to notice "the consternation which is occasioned among the different species of fowl" along Rydal Lake and to hear their "loud screams" [24] when an eagle strikes down among them; it is another to feel his own hands red. One who listens may hear in Wordsworth's poetry the "hungry Barkings" of the eagles; and he may also hear the poet's significant confession that he himself was an incarnate meance to the harmony of nature. Fundamental in the preparation for his life had been the early discipline by fear. The earliest distinction of any importance which his mind had made was that the beautiful was the good and the stealthy and destructive made up the evil. "At an early age, ere [he] had seen nine summers," this distinction was growing in his mind from seed which Nature had planted there. The seed was small, the growth was great. However trivial the incidents were out of which his imaginative knowledge of the forces of

---

[24] Wordsworth was, in fact, greatly interested in "internecine" eagles. He observed them not only in the "fair Cumberland" of Legouis, but in Ireland and in Switzerland. Their "hungry barkings" he has kept in his ode *On the Power of Sound*, v. 201, and otherwhere he notes their wide ravaging and the fact that even the horse is naturally afraid of the eagle.— See Grosart, *op. cit.*, pp. 101, 172, 312, and *The Borderers*, v. 1516.

life grew, the mind within which the incidents fructified was **extra**ordinarily fertile and strong. His deed may have been to catch woodcocks, to steal them from the springes of another, to rob bird's nests, or uninvited to go " alone into a Shepherd's boat " on Patterdale. The results from those deeds were loud dry whisperings of the wind telling him he did evil, and blank desertion, and oppressive dreams filled with " huge and mighty forms, that do not live like living men." That these experiences took on imaginative color through recollection many years later deepens their significance.

Remembering that in his " Earliest communings with nature " he had been shocked and shocked to the center of his mind, remembering that it was Nature who by her intimate discipline made him aware of good and evil, and that because of this discipline his mind had turned round " As with the might of waters," let us read again what he himself has written.

> If, in my youth, I have been pure in heart,
> If, mingling with the world, I am content
> With my own modest pleasures, and have liv'd,
> With God and Nature communing, remov'd
> From little enmities and low desires,
> The gift is yours; if in these times of fear,
> This melancholy waste of hopes o'erthrown,
> If, 'mid indifference and apathy
> And wicked exultation, when good men,
> On every side fall off we know not how,
> To selfishness, disguis'd in gentle names
> Of peace, and quiet, and domestic love,
> Yet mingled, not unwillingly, with sneers
> On visionary minds; if in this time
> Of dereliction and dismay, I yet
> Despair not of our nature; but retain
> A more than Roman confidence, a faith
> That fails not, in all sorrow my support,
> The blessing of my life, the gift is yours,
> Ye mountains! thine, O Nature! Thou hast fed
> My lofty speculations; and in thee,
> For this uneasy heart of ours I find
> A never-failing principle of joy,
> And purest passion.   *The Prelude*, II, 443-466.

This is in truth the whole course of Wordsworth's love for Nature, and this the witchcraft she has used upon him.

Wordsworth's mastery of the fear and melancholy occasioned by the dereliction of men was not gained without the shock of testing. When at the age of seventeen he went to Cambridge he found himself " begirt with temporal shapes Of vice and folly." His peasant ignorance exposed him to " an indefinite terror and dismay." He thought wretchedly of all the guilt of life. The sight of evil filled him with " dislike and most offensive pain," but he did not retreat from life. He resolved rather to try to understand life and the evil in it.

We still speak not too distinctily of the actual boy, but of the poet, being unwilling to distinguish between " naked recollection " and " after-meditation " where Wordsworth himself does not. No longer now " a transient visitant " in London he opened his mind to the variety of the scene. The city was in masquerade before him, and his eye was an inquiring one. Faces, faces passing in mystery before him, the face of the blind beggar, the face of the rosy babe and the demirep,

> The Comers and the Goers face to face,
> Face after face,—

he scrutinized them all. Before the showman's platform he stretched his neck and strained his eye and listened to the infernal din along with the crowd. The theatre was his delight, the theatre with its chaotic pageantry: the beauteous dame in the thick-entangled forest, the trumpeters and the king, the captive and the romping girl who " Bounced, leapt, and paw'd the air,"—he was enchanted with them all. Not so impressed was he with the comely bachelor who, " fresh from a toilet of two hours," ascended the pulpit, with seraphic glance looked up,

> And, in a tone elaborately low
> Beginning, lead his voice through many a maze,
> A minute course, and winding up his mouth,
> From time to time into an orifice
> Most delicate, a lurking eyelet, small
> And only not invisible, again
> Open[ed] it out, diffusing thence a smile
> Of rapt irradiation exquisite. *The Prelude*, VII, 549-556.[25]

Here where he had first heard " The voice of Woman utter blasphemy " and had first seen her in her trade with dissolute men, he listened and watched. But in the city he was beyond his element.

---

[25] Cf. Canto XXIX of Dante's *Paradise*.

3

He meditated too ardently upon the reconciliation of good and evil. A green speciousness permeates his persuasion that man is one and that the soul will pass through all nature and however wicked rest with God.

The experience gained in London, therefore, availed Wordsworth little in meeting happily the test of France. The passions of the time were imponderable, and he was of the time. If ever through confessed despair Wordsworth met the charge that he retreated in dismay from the world, it was precisely in his record of the days following the October of 1792. No one shall say that it is not a strange record we read; and no one can feel that the poet achieved that subtle candor which informs the silences of verse with confessional truth. I am astonished when I hear him say,

> No shock
> Given to my moral nature had I known
> Down to that very moment,

and I find that he does not refer to his desertion of Annette but rather to a subsequent event, England's declaring war upon France! Yet when I consider all that is implied in the statement that Wordsworth " too easily found refuge by reassuming the rather uncritical peace of mind he had known " in his adolescence, and that he too readily lightened the weight of life by a mystic mood, I am more astonished. " Through months, through years, ghastly visions of despair " assailed him. After a long and fearful purgation he had to begin to live again with such strength as he could. That ultimately, having suffered, Wordsworth was able to put away the desolation of death and stand up and lift the weight of the world is rather a manifestation of his power than an evidence of his weakness. The case is not one in which he knew no pain but rather one in which he mastered in part the grief with which he was acquainted.

> Most melancholy at that time, O Friend!
> Were my day-thoughts, my dreams were miserable;
> Through months, through years, long after the last beat
> Of those atrocities (I speak bare truth
> As if to thee alone in private talk)
> I scarcely had one night of quiet sleep
> Such ghastly visions had I of despair.
> *The Prelude*, X, 369-375.

Is this not enough? And if here there be a lack of candor in matters most intimate,

> The best of what we do and are
> Just God, forgive!

The secret happiness of a strong man is not had without a price. However fortunate Wardsworth's life may have been, there is evidence enough that as a man he paid in measure for the strength he had. Examined with an open mind, his poetry does not too often assure us that life is good. It is an uncritical mind indeed to which much of it brings a " healing peace." But in the best and master thing Wordsworth is sure: he is sure of the dignity of man and of the divinity of life. He is sure that an awareness of beauty is an evidence of things unseen. He will teach us at last what he has learned that it is sufficient for us to know:

> How the mind of man becomes
> A thousand times more beautiful than the earth
> On which he dwells, above this Frame of things . . .
> In beauty exalted.

University of Michigan.

WORDSWORTH: POET OF THE UNCONQUERABLE MIND

By Bennett Weaver

"Shine, Poet! in thy place, and be content. "

WORDSWORTH, said Arnold, "is one of the very chief glories of English Poetry." From the beginning his has been a "divine vitality." He himself was persuaded that he derived his light from heaven; and like Piccarda, who, though humbly placed, found her peace in God's will, Wordsworth, though not "pre-eminent in magnitude," was assured that the light which came to him was, for that reason, of no less divine origin. With this persuasion some of his contemporaries and some of ours are not in accord. Their reasons, of course, are greatly various. Yet it is noteworthy that certain of those characteristics which in his own time made him slow to be accepted, in our time tend to make him poorly read or not read at all. Hence it would seem that one might say something about the characteristics in question.

The first of these is originality. This characteristic is more likely to stir up opposition at first than in later times. "Whatever is too original will be hated at first," writes DeQuincey. Lamb finds Wordsworth bold in originality, offending the weak. He is "ambitious of originality," says Jeffrey, and holds that this will never do. His friend Wilson knew him to be "most original"; and Bradley later states that there is none more original than he: he is unique. Another poet offers us a cap for this:

> When God desires a man to fall,
> He makes him an original.

Wordsworth himself realized this truth. He wrote to Lady Beaumont: "Never forget what, I believe, was observed to you by Coleridge, that every great and original writer, in proportion as he is great or original, must create the taste by which he is to be relished." This paradox he put more neatly in *A Poet's Epitaph*:

> And you must love him, ere to you
> He will seem worthy of your love.

This is a hard saying, more than suggesting the "egotistical sublime" which offended Keats and might repel others. Yet here is something which insists upon itself, an originality having in it that pristine force which will make its way. The mind which voyages "through strange seas of thought, alone" may well fetch to port starry goods of rare worth.

This brings us to the second reason why Wordsworth was not popularly read in the early nineteenth century and is not now. The reason is that he deals with the elemental. The elemental alone may endure "the unimaginable touch of time"; our eyes are fixed upon quick change. The elemental is simple; we are sensitive to the complex. Wordsworth lays us "as we lay at birth / On the cool flowery lap of earth." But we are of an "iron time / Of doubts, disputes, distractions, fears." Ease? Although man has sought it through the centuries, how can we have ease, fretted as we are with the fevers of despair? Let us be straw men stacked upon a waste land. But within the straw let us find pathological agonies sufficient to make us aware of the significance of our utter insignificance. We will have our paradox, too. Wordsworth is interested in "the primary laws of our nature." There are those among us who prefer the Freudian chaos. Wordsworth is hale; they gather under the elms to savor disease. Wordsworth prefers "essential passions" which have attained maturity; they relish existential jejunity. Wordsworth writes of love; they want sex. He is at home and happy with the humble; they crave for the sophisticated. They thank god almighty in lower case for dying and not life. There is truly something different about them, but it is not elemental. The psychological, the pathological are not elemental; and the failure to see this truth has strongly tended to make their critical conclusions fantastic.

It is not that Wordsworth does not deal with madness; he does. But he treats it in a healthy way. It is, if one may quote Sir Andrew, "more natural." His mad mother may murder her own child, but she is neither an Abbie nor a Medea: not demoniac. Beneath a mountain thorn there is a little "hill of moss."

> I've heard the moss is spotted red
> With drops of that poor infant's blood;
> But kill a new-born infant thus,
> I do not think she could!

Yet she who sits beside that spotted grave is

> A Woman in a scarlet cloak,
> And to herself she cries,
> 'Oh misery! oh misery!
> Oh woe is me! oh misery!'

There are deserted women in Wordsworth, not like the apartment-dwelling "pure" women of Dorothy Parker who are astonished at being deserted, but natural women. There is Ruth who "loved not wisely but too well," in her elemental way. Like one of Hardy's maidens she is captured by a lovely youth in a military casque, a practitioner. Under his skilled touch her instincts warm, rise, respond. But after the response is complete he deserts her.

> God help thee, Ruth!—Such pains she had,
> That she in half a year was mad,
> And in a prison housed;
> And there, with many a doleful song
> Made of wild words, her cup of wrong
> She fearfully caroused.

Elemental passion—something experienced to make it real? Wordsworth had his Annette Vallon where Shakespeare had his Anne Hathaway, though Wordsworth deserted Annette and their child while the greater bard was true. Whether this gives Wordsworth the advantage of being more elemental than Shakespeare I shall not venture. I know of no one who has dealt with this matter more sanely than A. C. Bradley. Where Matthew Arnold says he "can read with pleasure and edification . . . everything of Wordsworth . . . except 'Vaudracour and Julia'," Bradley turns to that poem to enjoy a passage as elemental and lovely as are the description of Cleopatra and the breathings of Romeo. In truth, the lines of Wordsworth are of the same kind of poetry as are the lines of Shakespeare.

> The house she sat in was a sainted shrine;
> Her chamber-window did surpass in glory
> The portals of the dawn; all Paradise
> Could, by the simple opening of a door,
> Let itself in upon him. . . .
> A man too happy for mortality!

Bradley allows himself to smile at the poet's "reported statement that, had he been a writer of love-poetry, it would have been natural to him to write it with a degree of warmth . . . which might have been undesirable for the reader." But he recognizes the authentic, elemental quality of the lines.

Wordsworth's many studies "On Man and Human Life" are charged with the elemental. All we need remember is that there is about them nothing distortingly pathological. They are primary: nobly plain, bare, penetrating, profoundly sincere. As Arnold said, they have in them the permanence of "what is really life." There is Harry Gill with his troglodytish passion for property. There's the old Cumberland Beggar drawing men through sympathy to know that "we have all of us one human heart." There is Margaret who for seven years has waited the return of her son; and as she waits she cries out,

> My apprehensions come in crowds;
> I dread the rustling of the grass;
> The very shadows of the clouds
> Have power to shake me as they pass.

There are Michael, Isabel, and Luke—father, mother, child—set in the great eternal triangle. There is the youth of "Resolution and Independence" who, finding himself, loses his misery. There is brave Matthew, not "one of giant stature, who could dance / Equipped from head to foot in iron mail," and yet one who can frolic with sorrow. And there is that "Spirit fierce and bold," Robert Burns of "The piercing eye, the thoughtful brow, / The struggling heart." It was he—an elemental man if there ever was one—who showed Wordsworth "How Verse may build a princely throne / On humble truth." Standing beside his grave Wordsworth claims him friend: "Neighbors we were, and loving friends / We might have been." So Wordsworth again and again kept firm in his purpose, "truly though not ostentatiously" to trace "the primary laws of our nature."

A third reason for Wordsworth's being poorly read, perhaps more operative in our own time than formerly, is his celebration of nature. This reason takes on two phases: the first that which charges him with being a Romantic escapist; the second that which, because of the urbanization of our culture, holds him irrelevant.

In dealing with the charge that Wordsworth is an escapist, a happy warrior because he has retreated from battle, I must draw somewhat on what I have said in another place ("Wordsworth: The Property of Fortitude," *SP*, 4 Oct. 1940). Hazlitt himself made the accusation: "He calms the throbbing pulses of his heart, by keeping his eyes ever fixed on the face of nature. . . . No storm, no shipwreck startles us by its horrors: but the rainbow lifts its head in the clouds. . . . No sad vicissitudes of fate, no overwhelming castastrophe in nature deforms his page: but the dew-drop glitters on the bending flower, the tear collects in the glistening eye." Legouis follows Hazlitt, speaking of Wordsworth's "fair hills of Cumberland where no avalanche . . . is to be dreaded . . . where slumber lakes innocent." He makes no mention of the tale of William and Mary Watson, dashed to death over a cliff, or of the young man drowned in Grasmere. Kurtz follows Hazlitt, breathing bitterly against Wordsworth because he will not pursue death, because he is not shocked by the "internecine murder" to be observed in nature; yet the critic does not observe that the poet while describing his early dealings with nature nominates himself the murderer.

It may be sufficient to record here only a few facts touching this "spoiled child," as Hazlitt calls him, who had "no unruly and violent passions"; this too-happy child who, as Kurtz says, suffers from "an early disinclination and neglect vividly to envisage death." The truth is that Wordsworth's mother was especially concerned about the unruly and violent nature of her son, fearing his tendency "to drink wild water." But whatever his early disinclination to envisage death, at the age of eight he saw his mother dead, and his page carries the record of the catastrophe.

> Early died
> My honor'd Mother; she who was the heart
> And hinge of all our learnings and our loves:
> She left us destitute.

Cowper, remembering how it was with him when his mother died, says that we can scarcely "lay too much stress on the feelings of a child" caught in that primal tragedy. Horace Scudder, recording the fact that Keats's mother died while "he was still a boy," observes that "he grieved for her with the force of a passionate grief." How then of the passionate child, Wordsworth? And when he was thirteen his father died, and the family was broken up. "No sad vicissitude of fate, no overwhelming catastrophe." says Hazlitt. At twenty-two Wordsworth was fleeing France, leaving Annette and the baby Caroline. "No unruly and violent passions," says Hazlitt. And, says Hazlitt, "No storm, no shipwreck startles us with its horrors." But there was a storm and a shipwreck of startling horror: the beloved John was drowned.

Sea-Ship-drowned-Shipwreck-so it came,
The meek, the brave, the good, was gone;
He who had been our living John
Was nothing but a name.

In 1812 Wordsworth "lost two sweet children"; later death took his grandchild, "as noble a boy as ever was seen." Death took Dora, and he himself died breathing the words, "Going to Dora." The poet had no need to pursue death, for death pursued him. Ellis Yarnell found "the expression of his countenance sad, mournful; he seemed one on whom sorrow pressed heavily."

Perhaps enough of this. Yet the charge, whether in part fallacy or not, was not so much against the poet's life as against his page. Nothing in nature "deforms his page." A glance at some of the poems of the great decade should serve us here. Surely in *Guilt and Sorrow* Wordsworth has not neglected the "unruly and violent passions." Nor has he in *The Borderers*, which he himself called a study of "sin and crime." *Peter Bell* is hardly a flower poem, dealing as it does with a cunning, impudent man who, already having had twelve wives, lures away a sixteen-year-old girl, virtually to become her murderer and the murderer of her unborn child. The dominant theme of the poems of 1799 is death: death for the children of the village school, for Matthew's daughter, and for Lucy Gray,

The sweetest thing that ever grew
Beside a human door!

Here goes by a sexton with his wheel-barrow full of bones, finger joints and skulls to be piled in the boneyard. And here is star-like Lucy at last as starkly set as any dead thing in English literature.

No motion has she now, no force;
She neither hears nor sees;
Rolled round in earth's diurnal course,
With rocks, and stones, and trees.

The brooding upon sin, desertion, old age, and death continues until we are caught up by *The Prelude* which is gripped with wretched thoughts about the guilt of life. Remembering France alone Wordsworth writes:

> Most melancholy at that time, O Friend!
> Were my day-thoughts, my dreams were miserable;
> Through months, through years, long after the last
>   beat
> Of those atrocities . . .
> I scarcely had one night of quiet sleep
> Such ghastly visions had I of despair. (1805).

Was false, fleeting, perjured Clarence more horribly tortured? These words do not come from one who has turned his face from "the obvious facts of experience," but rather from one who, "Struggling in vain with ruthless destiny," cries,

> To life, to *life* give back thine ear:
> Ye who are longing to be rid
> Of fable, . . . hear
> The little sprinkling of cold earth that fell
> Echoed from the coffin-lid.

The second phase of the reason why Wordsworth's treatment of nature may leave certain readers uninterested is the urbanization of our culture. People who live in layers in apartment houses are not conditioned to care for the peace there is among the hills. The shows of earth and heaven are to them like "a landscape to a blind man's eye." For them the beauteous forms of nature cannot be recollected in tranquility. Theirs rather the "perpetual whirl / Of trivial objects." In his turn looking upon the shows of London the poet says,

> what a hell
> For eyes and ears! what anarchy and din
> Barbarian and infernal! 'tis a dream
> Monstrous in colour, motion, shape, sight, sound.

He was moved by

> the fierce confederate storm
> Of Sorrow, barricaded evermore
> Within the walls of cities.

If London is to be endured, he must throw over it "the beauty of the morning," a cloak of splendor such as the sun lays upon the hills of Cumberland. For this man, describing the moment of his dedication to poetry wrote:

> Magnificent
> The morning rose, in memorable pomp,
> Glorious as e'er I had beheld—in front

> The sea lay laughing at a distance; near,
> The solid mountains shone, bright as the clouds,
> Grain-tinctured, drenched in empyrean light.

This light does not shine upon the Brooklyn ferry or upon the "Stormy, husky, brawling—Hog-butcher of the world." No one needs condemn; but how shall he who lives where the fog comes in understand the empyrean light?

Yet it is not nature, it is the "Mind of Man" which Wordsworth claims as "the main region of [his] song." The fourth reason why the poet is poorly read is open before us: *Mind* connotes Philosophy, or for some readers Psychology; and Wordsworth in the modern sense is neither philosopher nor psychologist. He is therefore weighed on weighted scales and found wanting. The philosopher turns heavily away and the psychologist turns away. Wordsworth has already grown huffy with them, and quite unfairly perhaps.

> Physician art thou?—one, all eyes,
> Philosopher!—a fingering slave
> One that would peep and botanize
> Upon his mother's grave?

What needs to be kept in mind simply is that Wordsworth is a poet. Philosophers and psychologists, if they will, may find in his poems matter for their business. Indeed Wordsworth in his way to a great degree may reveal the workings of the mind, but he does so as a poet.

To his own hurt Wordsworth weds the Mind of Man to Nature and so takes upon himself double trouble. The reader who has been alienated by the poet's special interest in nature may now be twice offended. For Wordsworth strictly says that "the discerning intellect of Man" is "wedded to this goodly universe / In love and holy passion." And he exclaims, "How exquisitely the individual Mind . . . to the external World / Is fitted:—and how exquisitely too— / The external World is fitted to the Mind."

He stands, then, on the one hand receiving "organic pleasure" from the "real solid world of images" about him and on the other aware of ecstasy when "the light of sense / Goes out, but with a flash that has revealed / The invisible world." So he makes his home with infinitude, passing unalarmed

> Jehovah—with his thunder, and the choir
> Of shouting angels, and the empyreal thrones.

He rises into "glory immutable" where "the heaven of heavens is but a veil." And so at last he learns to know how the Mind of Man, "In beauty exalted . . . becomes / A thousand times more beautiful than the earth / On which he dwells."

Let us make a brief progress from that place where "The visible scene/Would enter unawares into his mind" to this place of ascension. There was at first about the poet a real world of "rocks, and stones, and trees," of mountains, lakes, and clouds. They were to him "an appetite." From them he drank in "A pure organic pleasure." But presently, as he says in his Fenwick Notes, he became "unable to think of external things as having external existence. . . . Many times while going to school have I grasped at a wall or a tree to recall myself from this abyss of idealism to reality." The condition is more strikingly revealed in those lines which record his experience after stealthily taking the shepherd's boat.

> For many days, my brain
> Work'd with a dim and undetermin'd sense
> Of unknown modes of being; in my thoughts
> There was a darkness, call it solitude,
> Or blank desertion, no familiar shapes
> Of hourly objects, images of trees,
> Of sea or sky, no colours of green fields;
> But huge and mighty Forms that do not live
> Like living men mov'd slowly through the mind
> By day and were the trouble of my dreams. (1805)

Under the stimulus of fear the mind is brought to "obstinate questionings / Of sense and outward things." The creative imagination is excited and exercised. A power is being developed that will turn "The mountain's outline and its steady form" to grandeur and to majesty. Through "the press / Of self-destroying, transitory things" the mind is coming to see immutable Beauty. Let desolation climb from low to high, Beauty shall not feel change or suffer "the unimaginable touch of Time."

We are now come to one of the great paradoxes of Wordsworth the paradoxical. We now shall speak of things which, "Through sad incompetence of human speech" must lie "far hidden from the reach of words." We are about to enter "an independent world/Created out of pure intelligence." We stand within one of those "spots of time" in which "The mind is lord and master—outward sense / The obedient servant of her will." And then, as "the light of sense / Goes out, but with a flash that has revealed / The invisible world" we come to know that "Our destiny, our being's heart and home, / Is with infinitude, and only there." Coming to know that his mind is "A thousand times more beautiful than the earth / On which he dwells," coming to know that he may make the world about him, living for him and for "the God who sees into the heart," man passes the choir of angels, "In beauty exalted."

A fifth reason why Wordsworth may not be picked up and attended to lies in the moral character of his poems. "There is scarcely one of my poems which does not aim to direct attention to some moral sentiment," he writes to Lady Beaumont. He purposes "to console the afflicted . . . to teach the young," to make man "wiser, better, and happier." He is aware that this purpose was offensive to the "wits and witlings" of his time. Holding that a poet was "a man speaking to men—rememberable things," he feels the importance of being earnest about his work. Joining with "the Man of science" he "rejoices in the presence of truth," and as jesting Pilate would not, he strives to make truth available to men. He is committed to meaning, and being so committed he is locked into the order of things. It is natural for him then, even necessitous to say that "love is an unerring light, / And joy its own security." Out of the agony of our times—and we have our agony—having no cure for our troubles but to set them upon "unyielding despair," we say again to Wordsworth, and sadly say it, "This will never do."

Yet we remember that his times and ours are greatly similar. The changes of his day surged with terror. War shook his world. Man marked the earth with ruin and marched upon "earthquake spoils" until the "crowning carnage, Waterloo." Wordsworth himself lost his sense and cried out: "Carnage is God's daughter!" Wellington came to the end of it all saying, "I thank God that I am spared the ruin that is gathering around us." That was like what William Pitt had said ten years before Napoleon fell: "There is scarcely anything around us but ruin and despair." Strange days in which to speak of love and joy!

But the morality of Wordsworth went down into his sonnets dealing with social and political matters. There must be, he says, not only "simplicity of style" but "grandeur of moral sentiment." For the subject of these poems is "civil liberty and national independence."—War and revolution, revolution making for freedom in America but leaping from tyranny to tyranny in France. Pointing to a hunger-bitten peasant girl beside a road near Orleans, the idealist Beaupuy said to his English friend, " 'Tis against *that* which we are fighting." But before the fight was over and the tumbrils quiet. Beaupuy was dead and Robespierre and Mirabeau had had their fling. Chill fear got hold of the heart of Burke; the dreadful horror of the time nearly broke the mind of Wordsworth. There were changes in England, too: the agricultural revolution and the industrial revolution came on. The rich became richer and more debased, and all were topped by a porcine royalty. Beggars roamed the land; the terrible prisons were stuffed; and many a Goody Blake labored seventeen hours a day, only to starve. Children were stolen from the streets of London to be fed into the mills of Manchester. Little girls of ten and twelve, with iron collars around their necks, were lurching through the mine shafts of Cornwall, dragging after them small baskets of coal. And the Church of England lifted its pontifical hand to bless the Status Quo. No time for a dry little ambivalent trick of verse.

> Milton! thou shouldst be living at this hour:
> England hath need of thee: she is a fen
> Of stagnant waters: altar, sword, and pen,
> Fireside, the heroic wealth of hall and bower,
> Have forfeited their ancient English dower
> Of inward happiness. We are selfish men.

England was indeed laying waste her powers. And again Wordsworth cries out,

> O Friend! I know not which way I must look
> For comfort, being, as I am, opprest,
> To think that now our life is only drest
> For show; mean handy-work of craftsman, cook,
> Or groom!—We must run glittering like a brook
> In the open sunshine, or we are unblest:
> The wealthiest man among us is the best:
> No grandeur now in nature or in book
> Delights us. Rapine, avarice, expense,
> This is idolatry; and these we adore:
> Plain living and high thinking are no more:
> The homely beauty of the good old cause
> Is gone; our peace, our fearful innocence,
> And pure religion breathing household laws.

What wonder that Wordsworth wrote, "by the soul / Only, the Nations shall be great and free." What wonder, thinking of the bloody food upon which Napoleon gorged, that he said,

> 'Tis not in battles that from youth we train
> The Governor, who must be wise and good.

And what wonder, turning to Toussaint L'Ouverture who was betrayed by the French, that he wrote

> Thou hast left behind
> Powers that will work for thee; air, earth, and skies;
> There's not a breathing of the common wind
> That will forget thee; thou hast great allies;
> Thy friends are exultations, agonies,
> And love, and man's unconquerable mind.

"Wordsworth's sonnets—beautiful—majestic—sublime," says John Wilson. What more can a poet do? What more—though there is more—shall we require? Not since Milton sang of the "Babylonian woe" have we had words of such power as these; and since, no such words.

We have now one final question to answer: is this all merely high discourse, magniloquence, orotund and mighty indeed, but no more? Is it poetry? Truly, is there in his words

> The light that never was, on sea or land,
> The consecration, and the Poet's dream?

We may have in him "an overflow of powerful feelings," but are these feelings ordered and wrought into artistic form by one who has "thought long and deeply"? Let the question persist a while, although in honest conscience we know that if it has not already been answered in what has been quoted there is nothing for it. As for false eloquence, was it not Wordsworth himself who proposed to write in "a selection of language really used by men"? Was it not he who, accused of being prosaic, nevertheless stoutly maintained that "some of the most interesting parts of the best poems will be found to be strictly the language of prose when prose is well written"?

Arnold wrote, "A single line is enough to show the charm of Chaucer's verse." Emerson wrote that if "Five lines lasted sound and true" the test of any poet had been met. Surely not only sound but having the accent of greatness is this characterization of *Job*: "the voice / That roars along the bed of

Jewish song." Again, words that have too often been wondered at to be disputed now, the description of the statue

> Of Newton with with his prism and silent face,
> The marble index of a mind for ever
> Voyaging through strange seas of Thought, alone.

Chatterton: "The sleepless Soul that perished in his pride." This thought upon Burns: "By our own spirits are we deified." For all men, this:

> There is
> One great Society alone on earth,
> The noble Living and the noble Dead.

or finally to shake us, these lines on the course of the French revolution; not

> false philosophy . . .
> But a terrific reservoir of guilt
> And ignorance filled up from age to age,
> That could no longer hold its loathsome charge,
> But burst and spread its deluge through the land.

Mighty lines, yes. But what of the mass of Wordsworth's work? Mass there is, nearly a thousand pages in any authentic edition. And let us admit that there is much which a Byron would find "drowsy, frowsy." Of a great deal that was written after 1808 we must ask, as Wordsworth himself does,

> Whither is fled the visionary gleam?
> Where is it now, the glory and the dream?

Our answer must be the one he gave. He found his mind grown "serious from the weight of life . . . its passions contracted." Except in extraordinary moments "the vision splendid" has faded "into the light of common day." It ill becomes us to charge against him what he charges against himself or to claim for him what he will not claim for himself. For him "The light that never was, on sea or land" has become "the light / Full early lost, and fruitlessly deplored. —

> 'Tis past, the visionary splendour fades;
> And night approaches with her shades.

Not having the poet's permission, then, to dispute some of the charges against him, I would on the basis of four passages alone claim him a "mighty poet." For quoting lines so familiar to Wordsworthians I seek excuse in the possibility that others may not know them well.

Was ever the reality of illusion more charmingly exploited than in these lines? "It is the thing! Behold!" as Andrea might say. The clock ticks to the heart, but it has not struck the hour when Wordsworth wrote

> She was a Phantom of delight
> When first she gleamed upon my sight;
> A lovely Apparition, sent
> To be a moment's ornament;
> Her eyes as stars of Twilight fair;
> Like Twilight's, too, her dusky hair;
> But all things else about her drawn
> From May-time and the cheerful Dawn;
> A dancing Shape, an Image gay,
> To haunt, to startle, and way-lay.

Then there is in the seventh book of *The Prelude* a description of St. Bartholomew's Fair for which one might challenge attention. Since the sentence is long I shall quote only a part of it. Standing on the showman's platform we see

> children whirling in their roundabouts;
> With those that stretch the neck, and strain the eyes,
> And crack the voice in rivalship, the crowd
> Inviting; with buffoons against buffoons
> Grimacing, writhing, screaming; him who grinds
> The hurdy-gurdy, at the fiddle weaves;
> Rattles the salt-box, thumps the kettle-drum,
> And him who at the trumpet puffs his cheeks,
> The silver-collar'd Negro with his timbrel,
> Egyptians, Tumblers, Women, Girls, and Boys,
> Blue-breech'd, pink-vested, and with towering
>   plumes . . .
> All out-o'-the-way, far-fetch'd, perverted things,
> All freaks of Nature, all Promethean thoughts
> Of Man; his dullness, madness, and their feats
> All jumbled up together to make up
> This Parliament of Monsters. (1805)

The next lines from the sonnet "It is a beauteous evening" have in them an image of purest loveliness.

> It is a beauteous evening, calm and free,
> The holy time is quiet as a Nun
> Breathless with adoration; the broad sun
> Is sinking down in its tranquility;
> The gentleness of heaven broods o'er the Sea:
> Listen! the mighty Being is awake,
> And doth with his eternal motion make
> A sound like thunder—everlastingly.

This contrast of the quiet of the nun "Breathless with adoration" with the everlasting thunder of the sea is artistry beyond praise.

Finally, to illustrate the power of Wordsworth's mind working in full glory I take the passage describing the gloomy strait through which he walked after he had crossed the Alps.

> The immeasurable height
> Of woods decaying, never to be decayed,
> The stationary blasts of waterfalls,
> And in the narrow rent at every turn
> Winds thwarting winds, bewildered and forlorn,
> The torrents shooting from the clear blue sky,
> The rocks that muttered close upon our ears,
> Black drizzling crags that spake by the way-side
> As if a voice were in them, the sick sight
> And giddy prospect of the raving stream,
> The unfettered clouds and regions of the Heavens,
> Tumult and peace, the darkness and the light—
> Were all like workings of one mind, the features
> Of the same face, blossoms upon one tree;
> Characters of the great Apocalypse,
> The types and symbols of Eternity,
> Of first, and last, and midst, and without end.

These lines speak trumpet-tongued. In their voice we hear the continuing power of Wordsworth's unconquerable mind.

University of Michigan